Angela Murrills

# Balls!

whitecap

For more information, contact Whitecap Books, 351 Lynn Av-
enue, North Vancouver, British Columbia, Canada V7J 2C4. Visit
our website at www.whitecap.ca.

All recommendations are made without guarantee on the
part of the author or Whitecap Books Ltd. The author and
publisher disclaim any liability in connection with the use
of this information.

*Edited by Joan Templeton*
*Proofread by Ann-Marie Metten*
*Design by Michelle Mayne*
*Food photography by Geoffrey Ross*
*Food styling by Ryan Jennings*

Printed in Canada

**LIBRARY AND ARCHIVES CANADA CATALOGUING
IN PUBLICATION**

Murrills, Angela
       Balls! : round the world fare for all occasions / Angela
Murrills.
Includes index.

ISBN 978-1-55285-867-7
ISBN 1-55285-867-7

1. Meatballs. 2. Cookery (Meat). I. Title.
TX749.M87 2007        641.6'6        C2007-901776-2

The publisher acknowledges the financial support of the
Government of Canada through the Book Publishing Indus-
try Development Program (BPIDP) and the province of British
Columbia through the Book Publishing Tax Credit.

*To Peter and Kate*

# Acknowledgments

Thanks to all the good friends in North America and France who have sat around tables with me in both countries and talked food—sparking ideas, and fueling debate and endless conversation.

A huge thank you to my agent provocateuse, Sally Harding, of The Harding Agency. This book would have gone no further than a flippant email if she hadn't leapt on the idea. Thanks to Joan Templeton of JET Editorial Services for finesse-ing the words, and Ryan Jennings and Geoffrey Ross for the fine photos.

Thanks to Taryn Boyd at Whitecap Books for walking me ever so patiently through which buttons to click during the editing process, and thanks of course to publisher Robert McCullough who agreed that a celebratory lunch was a perfectly reasonable request to include in a contract.

Finally, my heartfelt thanks to my nearest and dearest, Peter and Kate, for helping to make, helping to eat, and providing feedback on these spherical edibles.

# Contents

# Introduction

When you're cooking, thoughts meander and ideas arrive out of the blue. The inspiration for this book came somewhere between undoing a brown-paper-wrapped package of lean ground beef and serving up supper straight from the skillet. In between, I'd hauled out the trusty Cuisinart for breadcrumb-making and onion-chopping purposes, mixed in some herbs, and opened a can of tomatoes. It was all very relaxed and meditative. Just what you want at the end of the day.

That's the first thing to know about meatballs: they're undemanding. They don't call for obscure ingredients or split-second timing, which probably (I realized) explains why so many cultures have this global food: from Germany's sharply sauced *Königsberger klops* to the *bitterballen* they snack on in Amsterdam bars, to the various meaty nuggets, fragrant with cumin and other spices, that show up on laden tables around the Mediterranean. The thing was, if meatballs are so popular, how come they never make it onto posh menus? Simple. Posh ingredients don't lend themselves to ball form. Theoretically you could seek out perfectly formed Périgord truffles, but if you tried scooping neat globes of foie gras with your trusty melon baller (a gadget I'll get to on page 136) it would melt in your fingers.

Meatballs, on the other hand are fun to make—modeling clay for grownups. It feels good to scoop up some seasoned mixture and roll it between your palms. If you're alone, it shifts you into a contemplative mood. This is also where the whole family can meet over the kitchen counter. Not to be too sly, but kids who help make their own supper are far more inclined to end up eating it.

Meatballs aren't overly fussy about temperature either. Blow-on-your-fingers hot from the pan, or at room temperature, or cold the next day, they still taste good—which makes them (unsauced obviously) terrific food for picnics, lunch boxes, or road trips. In many countries they're street food. You stand around a little stall, charcoal smoke rising, waiting for the owner to scoop his meatballs off the grill into a piece of flatbread. In fact, it's odd that more Western fast food companies haven't roamed beyond the meatball sub.

From reminiscing about the many forms and flavors of meatballs I'd eaten, it was a short jump to thinking about other spherical foods. Flawless scoops of sorbet or ice cream. Satanically calorie-laden chocolate truffles. The rococo desserts, glistening with caramel, in the windows of French patisseries. But if these were the glamor side of the round world, there was also a dark side—in the shape of the many round foods (beginning with meatballs) that don't get the respect they deserve.

With a few exceptions—musky, flawless truffles come to mind— round vegetables are as far down the vegetable social scale as meatballs are on the carnivorous one. These days, tomatoes are only acceptable with the culinary cognoscenti if they are heirloom varieties and any other color but red. Beets or beetroot or silver beet, depending where you come from, the same. Plump, pale button mushrooms don't have the same cachet as porcini or chanterelles. How about turnips and rutabagas, the earthy paysans of the vegetable community? They rarely get invited to dinner parties. Frozen peas? Be serious. These recipes are.

They're also fast and easy to make. It's daunting to watch a TV chef throw together a meal for 10 in 30 minutes, including commercial breaks. What you have to bear in mind is that others have chopped, measured, sliced, and diced so that all you see on TV is basically an assembly job. But while this is not high-end fare that takes itself too seriously, it is food that's seriously good. And—like any dish, whether haute cuisine or, well, meatballs—good food starts with good ingredients.

Thrift isn't a topic that crops up much in foodie circles or chef-written cookbooks. Hands up, those who haven't been burned by the realization that two pounds of smoked sablefish Actually Costs Rather a Lot. One scallop dish apart (and it's worth the investment), all recipes here are economical. Consider the cost of a pound of ground beef compared to the same amount of steak. Look at ground lamb—it's a third the price of those expensive little racks. Then realize that the old-fashioned way of thinking, that a pound of protein—boneless beef or lamb, fish, or chicken—feeds two, needn't apply these days when we all want to put more veggies and grains on our plates. By and large, these recipes call for a pound of meat but they feed four. Finally, you can cook most of these dishes on top of the stove. Easier on your utilities bill. Easier on the planet.

But four servings? "What if there's only me, or me and my friend, or us and the three-year-old?" Like you, I've often wondered why, in a time of dwindling household sizes, most recipes are designed to feed four or even six. I've opted for four servings in most cases because doing the math is easy if you want to halve it. If you're on your own, do that and ask someone over, or have leftovers the following night.

I'll be honest. The book's title has provoked the odd giggle and the occasional outright splutter. But good taste prevailed (literally) and, while tempted, I didn't include recipes for Rocky Mountain

oysters, cowboy caviar, or barnyard jewels (or a whole lot of other euphemisms I found on the Internet). Equally, while I adore puns, I came up with only the names—not the recipes—for Jugged Hare Balls, Fried Cricket Balls, and an adaptation of the famous dish called *socca*, served in the back streets of Nice, because they didn't sound as though they would taste very good.

These are not three-star-restaurant dishes. This is easy, delicious food to make with love for yourself and the people you care about. Food that goes with conversation, discussion, and laughter as you all sit down at a table.

Preferably one that's round.

# Meatball Basics

## PRESENTATION IS EVERYTHING: WHAT THAT MEANS

When I was growing up in England, my mum used to serve poached cod with white sauce and mashed potatoes. One day she discovered chopped parsley and from then on you couldn't stop her. None of us can, or want to, emulate professional chefs who have a troop of kitchen minions tarting up plates behind the scenes before they're brought to table. Renegade chef Anthony Bourdain has a wonderful chapter in his *Kitchen Confidential* on how to make plates look professional. Thus, slightly with tongue in cheek, many recipes include suggestions for elevating your dish from the mundane to the photogenic so that your more obsessed foodie friends can record it for posterity with their digital cameras.

## A WORD ABOUT EQUIPMENT

Thoreau advised us to "beware of all enterprises that require new clothes." I'd say the same about recipes calling for new gadgets. Beyond a few sharp knives and some heavy pans, you don't need much. That said, I swear by the Cuisinart food processor I've owned since 1978, which, apart from needing minor parts replaced over the years, still merrily chugs along. The other devices I couldn't live without are a Microplane grater and a Donvier ice cream maker. Bypass buying the gadget du jour. Better to put your money into the best ingredients.

## WHAT MEAT TO USE

Beef, pork, or lamb—any ground meat usually costs less than buying, say, steaks or chops, so buy the best you can. Look for kindly reared animals whenever possible. Go to a real butcher rather than the supermarket. Buy several pounds (old-fashioned butchers still think in pounds) at a time, portion them out into 1-pound (500-g) packages, and freeze.

Look for unusual meats too, such as buffalo. Try turkey once in a while. Whenever you can, choose lean or extra-lean ground meat.

## REDUCING THE FAT

Unless they're exceptionally lean, your meatballs will ooze some fat as they cook in the skillet. Get rid of it with a turkey baster each time you turn them. That way they'll crisp better. Once the meatballs are completely cooked, discard any remaining fat before you proceed with the recipe.

## TESTING FOR FLAVOR

The instruction "season to taste" (almost always with salt and pepper) shows up in most cookbooks, including this one, and it means just that. Obviously you're not going to taste raw meatball mixture. Take a small spoonful of it, make it into a thin little patty (about the size of a quarter but thicker), cook it, and see what it tastes like.

In reality, most people don't do this. Cook with any regularity, and I think you have an instinct for how much salt and pepper is enough. Less is always better—your family and friends can always add more to the finished dish. If we're talking chilis, go easy the first time and see how the rest of the table responds. Again, you can always put out a bottle of hot sauce for real heat fanatics.

## SIZE DOES MATTER

One inch (2.5 cm) is a good size for a meatball in general. One technique that works is to use a ½ Tbsp (7.5 mL) measuring spoon: slightly heaped, it becomes a 1-inch (2.5-cm) meatball. In the course of meatball rolling, your attention may wander. As a result, size can increase without you noticing. Larger meatballs take longer to cook (which can mean you overcook the smaller ones). Do a size check midway through making a batch to be on the safe side.

## DRY BEFORE WET

Some meatball recipes call for chopping a number of ingredients. If you're using a food processor, do the dry ones (like bread or nuts) first. Then chop the onions, garlic, or ginger. Saves you having to wash out the bowl.

## BALL GOWNS: COATING YOUR MEATBALLS

Most meatballs are content to go naked into the skillet. Coating them with dry breadcrumbs or cornmeal can add extra crunch. Don't bother if they're going to be cooked with a sauce, as the outsides will soften.

## WHY MEATBALLS THRIVE ON BREAD, MILK, AND EGGS

Originally, including bread odds and ends in meatballs was probably intended both to use up stale loaves and to feed more people with less meat. Adding breadcrumbs does tend to lighten the mixture, especially if you soak the crumbs in milk first. Adding eggs helps firm up loose mixtures.

## CRUMBS! AND HOW TO MAKE THEM

Don't even think of buying breadcrumbs. If a dish calls for fresh ones, just use your loaf. Rip apart a slice or two, and either keep tearing (kids like to do this) to make the smallest possible pieces or whiz the torn pieces in a food processor.

Dry breadcrumbs are made from stale bread. If you don't have any, set a few slices of bread on a baking sheet in a low oven until they dry out. Then either use a food processor or put the dried slices in a plastic bag and bash them into crumbs with a rolling pin or wine bottle.

Unless a recipe calls for a specific type of bread, use whatever you have on hand. White, wholegrain, French baguettes, bread rolls, hot dog buns . . .

## USE A LIGHT HAND

Meatballs should not have the spring and bounce of their Ping-Pong cousins. Treat them gently, and don't squash the mixture together when you're combining ingredients. Use a wooden spoon and a gentle touch. Never, ever overcook. The contrast between crisp outside and tender interior is what you're after.

## ON TOP OR OUT OF SIGHT

Almost all the meatball recipes specify using a skillet on top of the stove. In most cases, you can also bake the meatballs on the center shelf of the oven at 375°F (190°C) for 30 minutes (or until cooked through), which is easier if you are making large quantities. Use a cookie cooling rack on a rimmed baking sheet, and discard the fat periodically. Once they're cooked, simply add them to the sauce if you're using one.

## FREEZING MEATBALLS

As long as the meat was fresh to begin with, you can definitely freeze the seasoned mixture (some flavors can intensify over time, so underseason to be on the safe side). You can also freeze individual meatballs on a baking sheet, then tumble them into a freezer bag. Thaw before cooking, and adjust seasoning if need be.

## ARE THEY COOKED?

With experience, you can touch a meatball, as you can a steak, and know if it's done. A better way is to cut one in half and see—there should be no hint of pinkness.

## A FINAL WORD

In one of my favorite books, *The Kitchen Diaries*, British writer Nigel Slater remarks: "A meatball never says, 'Look at me, aren't I clever?' It just says, 'Eat me.'" Exactly.

## Smart Starters and Super Soups

# Vodka Cranberry Merry-Go-Rounds

SERVES 4

1 cup (250 mL) vodka
1½ cups (375 mL) cranberry
   juice, chilled
1 splash of lime juice
8 to 12 fresh or frozen
   cranberries

*Thanks to the trend toward cosmopolitans and crantinis, tart, crimson cranberries now get star status year-round—not just at Christmas. Cranberry juice is sold everywhere, but you can't always track down the fresh berries. Bank a bag or two in the freezer and plop them into the drinks still frozen.*

(Chill the vodka, a cocktail shaker, and 4 martini glasses in the freezer for 1 hour before serving.)

Vigorously shake the chilled vodka, cranberry juice, and lime juice together in the cocktail shaker. Strain into the martini glasses, and drop 2 or 3 cranberries into each.

**"IT'S RED, IT'S ROUND, IT'S AFLOAT IN MY GLASS."**
If a maraschino cherry turns up in a cocktail, people tend to either eat it first or leave it till the server takes their glass away. If you're in the first group, just know that Oregon State University teaches a course called Maraschino Cherry 102, that delves into its history, science, and technology.

# Mountain High-Balls

12 ice cubes (approx.)
1 cup (250 mL) good whiskey
1 bottle glacier water, chilled

*Mixologist math: booze plus mixer equals high-ball. Could be a Scotch and soda, gin and tonic, or rum and cola. Nothing complicated about it. The name dates back to the era when railway authorities positioned a ball on a pole at the station to signal that the train was late. Presumably it became immortalized as a type of drink because a highball could be made so quickly, you could sink another one before the 7:10 took you home to the wife and kids.*

Place ice cubes in 4 highball glasses. Pour ¼ cup (60 mL) of whiskey into each. Add water to taste.

**WHY TO BUY HIGHBALL GLASSES**
Tall and narrow, the classic highball glass holds an 8- to 12-ounce (200- to 300-mL) drink. These are good for bloody Marys, bloody Caesars, and even orange juice. They also look very design-magazine-y lined up on the mantel with a single hot pink gerbera in each.

# Spinning Peaches

SERVES 4

1 small peach per person
1 bottle of bubbly

*My friend, food and wine writer Judith Lane, is famous for her inventive dinner parties, and it was she who introduced me to this wacky way to kick off a summer evening with appropriate style. Pour champagne if you're rich. Otherwise, any decent sparkling wine does the trick.*

Use brandy snifters or round-bowled wine glasses.

Wash, but do not peel, the peaches. Prick each one with a pin in about a dozen places.

Put a peach in each glass, then pour in the bubbly. Watch the peaches spin. Keep refilling the glasses as the levels drop.

When the bubbly is all gone, pull out the peaches, and peel and eat them.

**ANOTHER FUN DRINK: BUBBLE TEA**

This giggly beverage came to North America from Taiwan where it's a big hit with teens. The "balls" that give bubble tea its name are made of tapioca starch, which comes from the roots of the cassava (or manioc) plant. Shipped dried, the tapioca bubbles are reconstituted in sugar syrup. Some bubbles go in a glass with ice. A chilled drink goes in too, flavored with anything from mango to green lentils. Wide-gauge drinking straws let you slurp up the chewy bubbles one at a time

# Cocktail Meatballs

SERVES 6 TO 8

1 lb (500 g) lean ground beef
¾ cup (175 mL) finely chopped
   onion
1 egg, beaten
salt and pepper to taste
1 Tbsp (15 mL) cooking oil
2 Tbsp (30 mL) Thai sweet chili
   sauce
2 Tbsp (30 mL) lime juice
2 tsp (10 mL) finely chopped
   fresh ginger
lime rind slivers to garnish

*Most cocktail meatball recipes call for a chafing dish. Anyone still own one? Thought not. The modern solution is to bring the meatballs screaming hot from the oven. Easier still is to pick a recipe that still tastes good at room temperature. Needless to say, all full-sized meatballs can be made in miniaturized versions. The Thai sweet chili sauce I've suggested here is a favorite dip at Asian restaurants.*

Mix the ground beef, onion, and egg together in a large bowl. Season to taste. Roll into ¾-inch (2-cm) balls.

Heat the oil in a large non-stick skillet over medium heat. Brown the meatballs on all sides, about 10 minutes, or until cooked through. Drain on paper towels. Place in a heatproof bowl and keep warm.

Meanwhile, mix the sweet chili sauce, lime juice, and ginger in a medium-sized saucepan. Bring to a simmer over medium heat. Pour the sauce over the meatballs. Sprinkle with the lime rind.

Spear each meatball with a toothpick and serve immediately.

**PRESENTATION IS EVERYTHING**

In keeping with the Asian flavors used, you might want to put out small Chinese plates and bright scarlet chopsticks. Don't forget the paper napkins.

# The Big Cheese Ball

SERVES 6 TO 8

*A nostalgic throwback to the 1950s, this cocktail hour standard was originally intended to use up odds and ends of cheese languishing in the fridge. It still can, which is good to know if you're facing both the remnants of last night's expensive cheese platter and tomorrow night's guests. Use this recipe as a rough guide to quantities of hard and soft cheese—or make it from scratch. By all means, get rolling several days ahead of your next soirée, but leave the parsley sprinkling till just before serving.*

½ lb (250 g) cream cheese
¼ cup (60 mL) plain yogurt
½ cup (125 mL) shredded aged cheddar cheese
½ cup (125 mL) shredded Swiss cheese
1 Tbsp (15 mL) finely grated onion
1½ tsp (7 mL) horseradish
1½ tsp (7 mL) Dijon mustard
Worcestershire sauce or hot sauce to taste (optional)
⅓ cup (75 mL) chopped fresh parsley

Beat together the cream cheese and yogurt in a large bowl until smooth. Mix in the cheeses, onion, horseradish, and Dijon mustard. Sample a spoonful, and if the mixture needs more pep, add Worcestershire or hot sauce to taste. Cover with plastic wrap and chill until firm, about 1½ hours.

Several hours before you will be serving it, shape the mixture into a ball and sprinkle with the parsley. Wrap the cheese ball in plastic wrap and chill until 1 hour before serving. Remove from the fridge so it has time to soften a little.

**PRESENTATION IS EVERYTHING**
Stand your cheese ball at the center of a large plate, and ring it with an assortment of crackers. If they're in season, dot cherry tomatoes here and there.

# Tuscan Cream Cheese Balls

SERVES 6 TO 8

½ lb (250 g) cream cheese
¼ cup (60 mL) purchased or
   homemade pesto
½ cup (125 mL) sun-dried
   tomatoes in oil, drained and
   finely chopped
⅓ cup (75 mL) grated Parmesan
   cheese
¼ cup (60 mL) pine nuts

*Italy's vigorous flavors took chefs by storm in the '80s and home cooks were quick to follow. Other fads of the time like Pac-Man and Dallas have thankfully faded, but we still crave the zing of dark red, sun-dried tomatoes and the summery taste of basil. Make these little treats any time of year, but keep them refrigerated until an hour before serving or they'll slump unappealingly like oversize bottoms on bar seats. Leftovers (unlikely) are delectable spread on chunks of rustic bread or tossed with hot pasta.*

Beat the cream cheese and pesto together until smooth. Fold in the sun-dried tomatoes, Parmesan cheese, and pine nuts until evenly mixed. Form into ¾-inch (2-cm) balls. Place on a waxed-paper-covered plate and chill.

Insert a toothpick into each one before serving.

**PRESENTATION IS EVERYTHING**

If you have a dark green plate, now's the time to bring it out.

**THE CASE FOR REAL PARMESAN**

Shop in the right places—and that means Italian delis—and you can buy authentic Parmigiano Reggiano with the telltale, pin-pricked rind for the same price as that orange-colored dust. Get the biggest hunk you can afford: I usually invest in a kilogram at a time, cut it into smaller chunks, wrap each one in plastic and then cooking foil, and freeze. Even when it's as hard and shiny as soap, Parmesan still grates well with your invaluable Microplane. Hang on to the rinds, too. Bury them deep in pots of bean or vegetable soup to add extra flavor and substance.

# New York Deli Balls

*Technically I should be using lox (which is salt-cured) in these deli balls, but lox is not as easy to track down as smoked salmon. You don't need flawless slices. Less expensive trimmings are fine. Roll these tidbits in breadcrumbs at the last possible minute or their overcoats will get unappealingly soggy. Though it goes against the very nature of this book, you can also whack the mixture into a bowl, smooth the top, and serve it with bagel chips (see sidebar).*

½ lb (250 g) cream cheese
½ lb (250 g) smoked salmon, coarsely chopped
1 Tbsp (15 mL) finely chopped red onion
1 Tbsp (15 mL) finely chopped parsley
1 Tbsp (15 mL) small capers, drained (approx.)
1 tsp (5 mL) lemon rind
1 cup (250 mL) fine fresh rye breadcrumbs
lemon wedges to garnish

Beat the cream cheese in a bowl until smooth. Fold in the salmon, onion, parsley, capers, and lemon rind. Form into ¾-inch (2-cm) balls, and refrigerate until just before serving.

Roll the deli balls in the breadcrumbs until coated. Garnish with the lemon wedges and more capers.

### PRESENTATION IS EVERYTHING

What with the vivid yellow of the lemon, the peachy-pink of the balls, and the bottle-green capers, a plain white plate looks best. If you can find one of those diner-style plates with the jagged-green-patterned rim, your deli balls will look fashionably retro.

### BAKING BAGEL CHIPS

You can buy bagel chips, of course, but why would you when it's so easy to make your own? Use day-old (or even older) bagels, slicing each one horizontally as thinly as possible. Try to get at least 8 slices from each bagel. Place in a single layer on a baking sheet. Brush lightly with olive oil. Bake for 20 minutes or until lightly browned at 325°F (160°C). Serve whole or snap into chips just before serving.

# Swedish Smoked Mackerel Balls

SERVES 6 TO 8

½ lb (250 g) cottage cheese
½ lb (250 g) smoked mackerel
    fillets
1 Tbsp (15 mL) chopped fresh
    dill
1 tsp (5 mL) freshly ground
    pepper, or to taste
rye or pumpernickel bread

*With its full-flavored flesh, mackerel is one of the undersung heroes of the underwater world, and smoked, it's fantastic. It also freezes well. Keep a package on hand and you can make these up very quickly. They're quite rich, so team them with small slices of rye or other dark bread thinly spread with cream cheese. Shots of aquavit maybe?*

Beat the cottage cheese in a large bowl until smooth. Use a fork to scrape the mackerel flesh off the skin into another bowl. Flake the fish (watching out for, and removing, any bones), add to the cottage cheese, and mash together until well blended, or whiz in the food processor. Mix in 2 tsp (10 mL) of the dill and add the pepper. Shape into ¾-inch (2-cm) balls. Chill until serving time.

Arrange on a platter and spike with toothpicks. Arrange triangles of rye bread around the edge and sprinkle the smoked mackerel balls with the remaining dill.

PRESENTATION IS EVERYTHING

Put a pot of pickled cornichons—authentically French if you can find them—or dill pickle spears at the center of the plate, then arrange the mackerel balls around them. Edge the plate with bread triangles or whole, cocktail-sized slices of bread.

# Minty Lamb Meatballs with Sweet-Sharp Dipping Sauce

SERVES 6 TO 8

*The classic combination of lamb aromatic with mint and garlic becomes the foundation for tasty little nibbles. Nobody wants to be stuck in the kitchen while the fun proceeds, so gather everyone around the stove and let them dive on your offerings the moment they're ready. Cranberry and apple jellies vary in sweetness. Adjust judiciously with lemon juice, and taste the sauce repeatedly until you get that fine balance between sweet and sharp.*

1 lb (500 g) ground lamb
1 egg, beaten
1 Tbsp (15 mL) chopped fresh mint
1 tsp (5 mL) finely chopped garlic
salt and pepper to taste
⅓ cup (75 mL) vegetable oil
¼ cup (60 mL) brown sugar
¼ cup (60 mL) lemon juice (approx.)
2 Tbsp (30 mL) water
2 tsp (10 mL) cornstarch
¼ cup (60 mL) cranberry or apple jelly
1 Tbsp (15 mL) Worcestershire sauce

Mix together the ground lamb, egg, mint, and garlic in a bowl. Season with the salt and pepper. Flour your hands and roll the mixture into ¾-inch (2-cm) balls.

Heat the oil in a large skillet over medium-high heat. Add the meatballs. Cook for about 12 minutes, turning occasionally, until they are golden, crisp, and cooked through.

While the meatballs cook (or beforehand), make the dip. In a small saucepan, whisk together the brown sugar, 2 Tbsp (30 mL) of the lemon juice, the water, and the cornstarch until smooth. Whisk in the jelly and Worcestershire sauce. Bring to the boil over low heat, and cook, stirring frequently, until thickened. Add up to 2 Tbsp (30 mL) more of the lemon juice to taste. Keep warm.

Pour the sauce into a small bowl and place at the center of a platter or plate. Surround with the meatballs. Insert a toothpick in each meatball. Serve immediately.

**PRESENTATION IS EVERYTHING**
Tuck a few small sprigs of mint around the edge of the platter.

**HOW MUCH JUICE IN A LEMON?**
A useful thing to know is that an average-sized and reasonably juicy lemon will give you about ¼ cup (60 mL) of juice. Rollin the lemon around on counter bef it unlea amount.

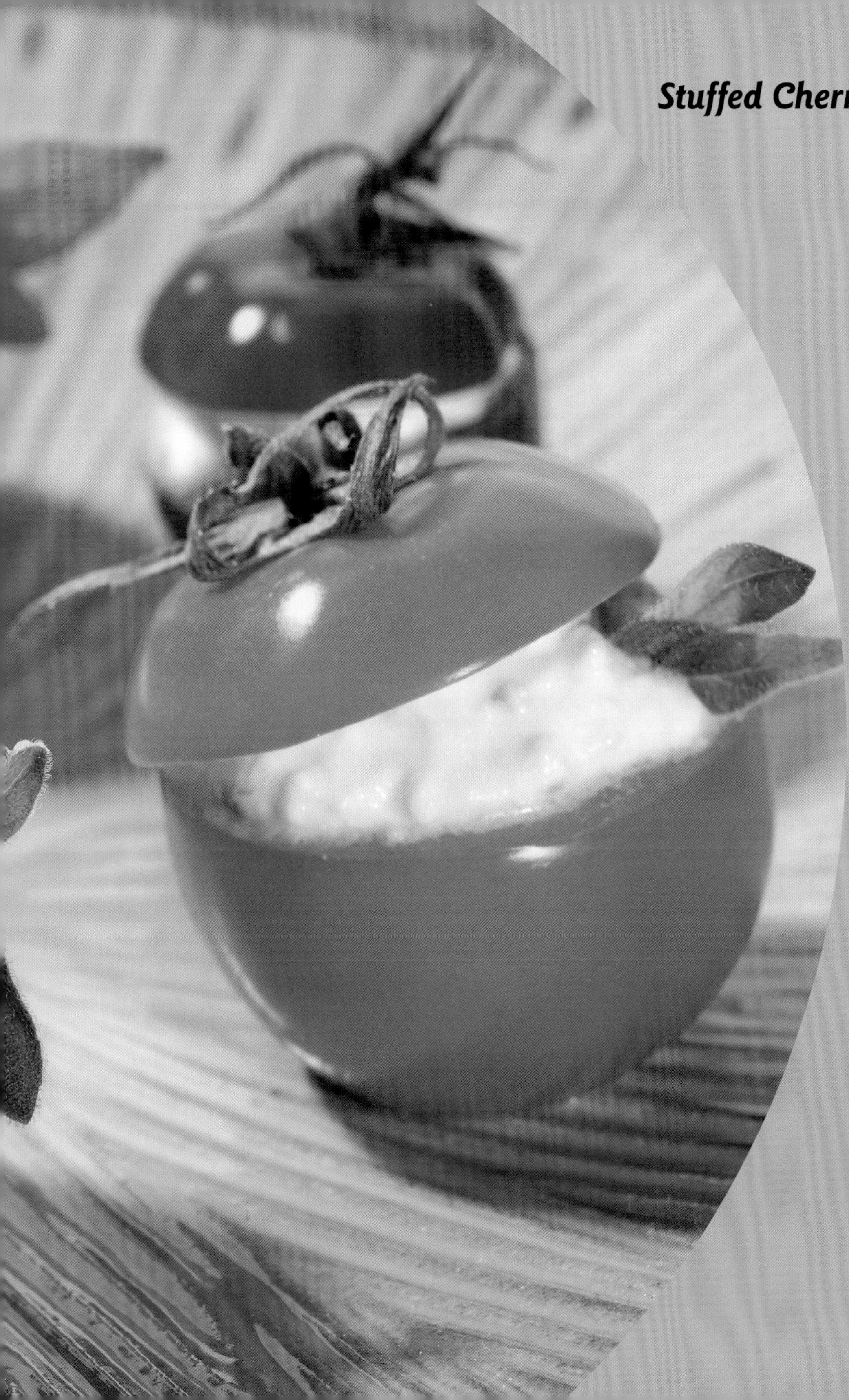

## Stuffed Cherry Tomatoes

# Stuffed Cherry Tomatoes

SERVES 6 TO 8

2 cups (500 mL) cherry
   tomatoes
1½ cups (375 mL) feta cheese
plain yogurt or milk (optional)
2 tsp (10 mL) dried oregano
fresh parsley or oregano sprigs
   for garnish

*A surgically sharp knife, a spoon to scoop out the innards, and time are all it takes to assemble these taverna-inspired nibbles. Don't make it hard on yourself by using the tiniest tomatoes you can find, but do try to buy them all in the same size range. Choose the creamy kind of feta cheese, not the crumbly sort. If it's not smooth enough, loosen it up with a bit of plain yogurt or milk.*

Slice the top off each tomato with a sharp knife, saving the caps. Scoop out the seeds and flesh with a spoon. Leave upside down on a plate to drain for 5 minutes.

Meanwhile, mash the feta cheese until smooth (you want it to be about the same consistency as cream cheese). Add yogurt if necessary to smooth it out. Add the oregano and mix well. Fill each tomato with a small dollop of the feta mixture. Replace the "lids."

Garnish the plate with parsley sprigs and refrigerate until serving time.

**PRESENTATION IS EVERYTHING**
Continue the "I must be in Corfu" feel by arranging these Greek nibbles on a simple pottery plate and serving grilled olives (see page 30) alongside.

**CHERRY TOMATOES GET STUFFED IN VARIOUS WAYS**
If you're short of time, substitute tapenade, either homemade or store-bought. Sun-dried tomato pesto is another piquant possibility.

# Puerto Vallarta Beach Balls

SERVES 6 TO 8

*All those seven-layer dips, guacamole, salsa, and chips that conjure up searing heat, cerulean skies, and frosty beers. How we love them. Here, all your favorite Mexican flavors get together in many little beach balls. You can also add chopped cilantro, but be careful. People either love this herb to the point of obsession, or think it tastes like soap and go nuts trying to pull every last little leaf out of your creation.*

**1 Tbsp (15 mL) vegetable oil**
**¼ cup (60 mL) finely chopped onion**
**1 tsp (5 mL) finely chopped garlic**
**one 19-oz (540-mL) can of black beans, drained, rinsed, and dried on a paper towel**
**1 Tbsp (15 mL) taco seasoning mix (see below)**
**1 pinch of cayenne pepper, or to taste**
**1½ cups (375 mL) coarsely crushed taco chips**
**2 Tbsp (30 mL) chopped cilantro (optional)**
**lime wedges for garnish**

Heat the vegetable oil over medium heat in a skillet. Add the onion and garlic. Cook, stirring frequently, until the onion and garlic are soft, about 5 minutes. Continue cooking the mixture until it's as dry as possible (5 to 7 minutes longer).

Meanwhile, whiz the black beans in a food processor until roughly chopped. Scrape in the onion and garlic mixture, and add the taco seasoning mix and cayenne. Pulse until the mixture is mostly smooth with some lumps remaining (you don't want a purée). Scrape out into a bowl.

Dampen your hands and shape the mixture into ¾-inch (2-cm) balls. Roll in the taco chip crumbs. Garnish with chopped cilantro (if using) and wedges of lime. Serve immediately.

**PRESENTATION IS EVERYTHING**

If this is the prelude to an all-Mexican dinner, now's the time to set the table with that parakeet-bright serape you bought from a beach vendor in a margarita-fogged moment.

## Taco Seasoning Mix   MAKES ABOUT ½ CUP (100 ML)

*Mixing up a batch of your own taco seasoning lets you go hot, super hot, or incandescent with spices.*

**2 Tbsp (30 mL) chili powder**
**2 Tbsp (30 mL) paprika**
**4½ tsp (22 mL) ground cumin**
**1 Tbsp (15 mL) garlic powder**
**cayenne pepper to taste**

Combine and store in a lidded jar.

# Those Bloody Cherry Tomatoes

SERVES 6 TO 8

cherry tomatoes
vodka
sea salt
3 shot glasses
toothpicks

*Treat even a single cherry tomato plant with minimal kindness and it rewards you with a bountiful crop. Why do you think one variety is called "Sweet 100"? But over-abundance is no bad thing (see page 113 for another idea). Essentially the elements of a Bloody Mary reconfigured, this is the simplest imaginable tidbit to nibble on a hot summer night when you don't have the energy to cook. I haven't indicated quantities. Just set out as many cherry tomatoes as you have, and top up the vodka and salt as needed.*

Pour the vodka into one of the shot glasses and place it at the center of a plate or platter. Pour the salt into another shot glass and position beside the first. The toothpicks go in the third shot glass. Arrange the tomatoes around the shot glasses.

Each person impales a tomato on a toothpick, then dips it in the vodka and then in the salt—experimenting until they come up with the right technique or supplies run out, whichever comes first.

**PRESENTATION IS EVERYTHING**

Obviously a mix of tiny red and yellow, obscure heirloom varieties elevate this into a dish even the loftiest gourmet won't scoff at.

# Gorgeous Gougère

SERVES 6 TO 8

*Warm, light, and cheesy, these little puffs are a classic French accompaniment to aperitifs and complete no-brainers to make. The same technique works for choux pastry (see page 32) and that's the starting point for all kinds of sweet and savory delights.*

1 cup (250 mL) water
½ cup (125 mL) butter
¼ tsp (1 mL) salt
1 cup (250 mL) flour
4 eggs
1 cup (250 mL) shredded Swiss cheese
1 Tbsp (15 mL) Dijon mustard
1 Tbsp (15 mL) finely chopped green onion

Preheat the oven to 425°F (220°C).

Combine the water, butter, and salt in a large saucepan over medium heat and bring to a boil. Remove from the heat, and add all the flour at once, beating well with a wooden spoon until it is thoroughly mixed. Place the pan back on the stove, and cook until the dough starts to pull away from the sides of the saucepan. Remove from the heat and beat the eggs in one by one. Gently stir in ⅔ cup (150 mL) of the cheese, the mustard, and the chopped green onion.

Using a 1-Tbsp (15-mL) measure, drop the gougère mixture onto an ungreased, rimmed baking sheet about 1½ inches (4 cm) apart. Sprinkle with the remaining ⅓ cup (75 mL) cheese.

Bake for 15 minutes. Lower the temperature to 400°F (200°C) and continue to bake for 15 minutes, or until golden brown and puffed. Serve warm.

PRESENTATION IS EVERYTHING

You can also drop these on the baking sheet to form a ring, in which case you can stand a small container of cornichons in the middle when serving. Rolled slices of prosciutto secured with toothpicks go nicely too.

# Grilled Olives en Brochette

SERVES 6 TO 8

2 cups (500 mL) black Greek
  olives, pitted
toothpicks

*Skewered cooked olives are another outrageously easy idea, but an excellent one that I first tasted in Crete with our friends Harry and Thea Prinianakis (after which, we ate a whole sheep on a stick). Heating olives really brings out the depths of their flavor. You can cook these on the barbecue too, handing them out as they're ready.*

Impale the olives in fours on toothpicks.

Either pop them on the barbecue for a few minutes, or cook them in a preheated, non-stick skillet until slightly browned in patches and warmed through. Serve immediately.

### PRESENTATION IS EVERYTHING

In keeping with their Greek heritage, serve these olives on a plate covered in fresh vine leaves (it's worth planting a vine in your garden solely for situations like these). Black and glossy, spitted olives also look dazzling on a scarlet or turquoise plate.

# Mon Petit Choux

MAKES 20

¾ cup (175 mL) water
⅓ cup (75 mL) butter
1 pinch of salt
½ cup (125 mL) flour
3 eggs

*The easy puff pastry base for dozens of fillings: ice cream or stiffly whipped cream for desserts; or a cream cheese-based mixture (smoked salmon? pesto?) for a quick cocktail snack.*

Preheat the oven to 400°F (200°C).

Combine the water, butter, and salt in a large saucepan over medium heat and bring to a boil. Remove from the heat, and add all the flour at once, beating well with a wooden spoon until it is thoroughly mixed. Place the pan back on the stove and cook until the dough starts to pull away from the sides of the saucepan. Remove from the heat and beat the eggs in one by one.

Using a 1 tsp (5 mL) measure, drop the choux pastry onto an ungreased, rimmed baking sheet.

Place on the top shelf of the oven. Bake for 15 minutes (don't open the door). Lower the temperature to 275°F (140°C) and continue to bake for 12 minutes. The little puffs should be golden brown and sound hollow when you tap them.

# French Meatball and Onion Soup

SERVES 4

*A stomach- and spirit-warmer, this soup is deeply satisfying on a winter's night, when you've just come in from the cold and have that snug feeling of knowing you don't have to go out again. Make the base for this traditionally inspired French dish ahead of time to mellow its flavors. As served to starving Parisian market porters, the authentic version is topped with melted cheese on toast. Here I've swiped one of the accompaniments to French fish soup: croûtes (little toasts) topped with cheese. There's cheese in the meatballs too.*

2 Tbsp (30 mL) butter
1 Tbsp (15 mL) vegetable oil
6 cups (1.5 L) thinly sliced onions
2 Tbsp (30 mL) flour
1 cup (250 mL) dry white wine
4 cups (1 L) beef stock
1 sprig of fresh thyme, or 1 tsp (5 mL) dried thyme
1 bay leaf
salt and pepper to taste
½ lb (250 g) ground beef
⅓ cup (75 mL) finely chopped onion
¼ cup (60 mL) chopped lean bacon
1 egg
1 tsp (5 mL) dried thyme
½ tsp (2 mL) dried oregano
½ tsp (2 mL) dried basil
½ tsp (2 mL) finely chopped garlic
⅓ cup (75 mL) fine fresh breadcrumbs
⅓ cup (75 mL) grated Parmesan cheese
1 Tbsp (15 mL) vegetable oil
½ baguette, cut in ½-inch (1 cm) slices, toasted both sides
1 cup (250 mL) grated Swiss cheese

Heat the butter and oil together in a large skillet over medium heat. Add the onions, reduce the heat, and cook until soft and golden, stirring occasionally, about 7 to 10 minutes. Sprinkle with the flour, stir well, and cook 5 minutes longer. Pour the wine into the skillet and stir.

Transfer the onion mixture to a saucepan. Add the stock, herbs, salt, and pepper, bring to a boil, and simmer for 20 minutes. Remove the herbs and refrigerate the soup base until needed.

Mix the beef, onion, bacon, egg, seasonings, breadcrumbs, and cheese together in a bowl. Season to taste with more salt and pepper. Form into ¾-inch (2-cm) balls.

Heat the oil in a skillet, and brown the balls on all sides, about 10 minutes. Remove to a plate lined with paper towels.

Bring the soup base to a simmer over medium-low heat. Add the meatballs and continue simmering until they are heated through.

Ladle into pre-warmed bowls, and serve the baguette toasts and grated cheese on the side.

## PRESENTATION IS EVERYTHING

For that instant *rive gauche* bistro ambiance, use deep pottery bowls to keep the soup hot to the last drop. Serve the toasts in a napkin-lined wicker basket and the cheese in a small bowl. *Bon appétit.*

# French Canadian Pea Soup

# French Canadian Pea Soup

SERVES 4 WITH LEFTOVERS

1 meaty hambone
2 cups (500 mL) dried green or
    yellow split peas, rinsed
1 cup (250 mL) chopped onion
¾ cup (175 mL) chopped carrot
½ cup (125 mL) chopped celery
1 tsp (5 mL) chopped garlic
1 bay leaf
salt and pepper to taste
water to cover

*Broke and living in Montreal, my friends and I survived on chunks of chemical-laden mystery meat and a culinary abomination called "hamburger toast." Also Habitant canned Québécois pea soup (peas are round, okay?) until we found we could cook it ourselves. This belly-warming recipe makes lots and lots, but it freezes well (although you may need to thin it with water when you reheat it).*

Put all of the ingredients in a large soup pot. Cover with the water, bring to a boil, reduce the heat, and simmer until the peas and vegetables are completely cooked and the meat is falling from the bone, about 2 hours.

Using kitchen tongs, pull out the hambone and set it aside to cool. Remove all the meat, discarding any skin or excess fat, and cut into ½-inch (1 cm) chunks. Set aside.

Remove the bay leaf from the soup. Using a blender, hand-held blender, or food processor, blend the soup to a thick purée. Return it to the soup pot, add the cubes of ham, and reheat, thinning the soup with water if it looks too thick.

PRESENTATION IS EVERYTHING

This is when to pull out the lidded soup tureen. Otherwise, cook this hefty potage in a two-handled pot and bring it bubbling to the table. Have that placemat ready. Quebec brews some extraordinary beers. A few of those, some crusty bread, and plenty of *joie de vivre* should do it.

# Matzo Ball Soup

SERVES 4

*Making authentic matzo ball soup is a lengthy and arduous process. This is an attempt to capture the spirit of the original. Jewish mothers will descend on me in droves and high dudgeon because I've left out elements like grebenes (chicken skin) and schmaltz (chicken fat), and I don't use a whole chicken. But at least it's not boneless, skinless chicken breast—it's moist, meaty, flavorful thighs.*

2 lb (1 kg) skinless, boneless chicken thighs, cut into ¾-inch (2 cm) pieces
1 cup (250 mL) coarsely chopped onion
water to cover
1 cup (250 mL) sliced carrots
½ cup (125 mL) thinly sliced celery
salt and pepper to taste
1 egg, beaten
1 Tbsp (15 mL) vegetable oil
¼ cup (60 mL) matzo meal (see sidebar)
½ tsp (2 mL) salt
2 Tbsp (30 mL) chicken broth
½ cup (125 mL) chopped fresh dill

Place the chicken and onion in a large saucepan, and cover them with the water. Bring to a boil, reduce the heat, and simmer for 15 minutes.

Add the carrots and celery, and continue simmering for 15 minutes longer. Remove from the heat and season to taste.

Whisk together the egg and vegetable oil in a large bowl. Add the matzo meal and salt, and mix well together. Mix in the chicken broth. Cover the bowl and refrigerate the mixture for 20 minutes.

Bring the soup to a boil over medium-high heat. Reduce the heat so that the soup is bubbling gently. Using a ½-Tbsp (7 mL) measure, scoop balls of the matzo mixture, approximately 1-inch (2.5 cm) in size, into the soup. Add the dill. Cover and cook for 30 minutes without removing the lid.

**PRESENTATION IS EVERYTHING**

A big soup tureen and a ladle—this is homey fare with nothing designer about it. Okay, a little sprig of dill on each serving if you must.

**MATZO MEAL**

. . . is merely ground-up matzo bread, the unleavened bread served during Passover. The most likely places to find it are ethnic grocery stores and delis. Mainstream supermarkets often carry matzo meal during Passover.

**JUST SO YOU KNOW**

Unused to traditional Jewish cuisine, Marilyn Monroe was somewhat disconcerted when, at a dinner party, she was served matzo ball soup for the first time. Her question to the table at large in that distinctively soft husky voice: "Do you eat any other parts of the matzo?"

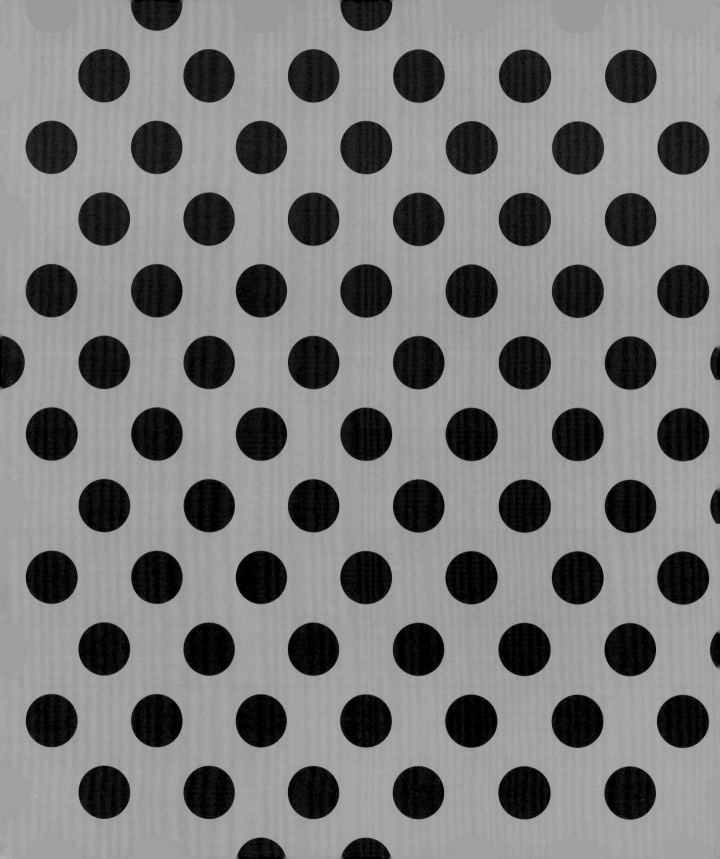

# Meatballs, Basic and Otherwise

# Spaghetti and Meatballs

SERVES 4

¼ cup (60 mL) fresh
   breadcrumbs
¼ cup (60 mL) milk
1 lb (500 g) lean ground beef
1 egg, beaten
⅓ cup (75 mL) finely chopped
   onions
⅓ cup (75 mL) chopped parsley
1 tsp (5 mL) dried basil
½ tsp (2 mL) finely chopped
   garlic
¼ tsp (1 mL) dried cinnamon
1 pinch of allspice
salt and pepper to taste
1 Tbsp (15 mL) olive oil
3 cups (750 mL) bottled,
   tomato-based pasta sauce
   (see sidebar)
1 lb (500 g) spaghetti, cooked

*In some Italian restaurants, you can find your-self facing a single meatball the size of a fist. No thanks. And then there's that song about "One Meat-ball." Again, no thanks. Apart from the off-putting task of cutting your way through it, that big a lump of meat isn't appetizing. Besides, small meatballs cook faster. You can freeze these meatballs, cooked, on a cookie sheet covered with plastic wrap, then tumble them into a plastic bag. Thaw (another reason for making them small) and reheat in store-bought pasta sauce while the pasta cooks.*

Soak the breadcrumbs in the milk for 5 minutes. Place all the remaining ingredients (except the salt, pepper, olive oil, pasta sauce, and pasta) in a large bowl, add the breadcrumbs, and mix thoroughly but gently. Season to taste with the salt and pepper. Form into 1-inch (2.5-cm) meatballs.

Heat the olive oil in a non-stick skillet over medium heat. Cook the meatballs, turning frequently, until they are browned on all sides. Drain on paper towels.

Remove any fat from the skillet and pour in the pasta sauce. Add the meatballs, and cook over medium-low until the sauce is simmering and the meatballs are heated through. Serve over the cooked pasta.

### PRESENTATION IS EVERYTHING

This is family fare. Lily-gilding isn't necessary. A little chopped parsley on each serving and a bowl of grated Parmesan on the table is enough.

## PASTA SAUCE IN A JAR

Of course, you can make tomato sauce from scratch but, to be honest, I haven't for years. Not when I can buy it ready to use—plain and simple, or with mushrooms or olives or spinach added—and it tastes so close to homemade. Get organic when you can.

*Why cobblestones? Because as the top layer of pasta cooks, it softens, forming little indentations between the bumps of the meatballs. When every supermarket sells frozen lasagna, yours has to be a bit different to avoid accusations of "look who's been to Costco again." Meatballs make the difference here. Please note that lasagna pans differ in size. You may have ingredients left over, or your lasagna may not come right up to the rim. This recipe is based on using a classic Pyrex 12 cup (3 L) pan.*

Preheat the oven to 350°F (180°C).

Bring 20 cups (5 L) of water to a boil in a large pot. Add the lasagna noodles and cook till they are soft but still firm, about 10 minutes (they will continue to cook in the oven). Drain the noodles and lay them flat in a single layer to dry on a dish towel.

Brush the bottom of the baking pan with a thin layer of pasta sauce. Set aside ½ cup (125 mL) sauce and combine the rest with the meatballs. Set down a layer of noodles on top of the sauce so that they touch but do not overlap. Top with approximately one-half the ricotta, one-half the mozzarella, and ⅓ cup (75 mL) of the Parmesan. Spoon half the meatball-and-sauce mixture on top.

Repeat once more with noodles, cheese, meatballs, and sauce. Top with the final layer of noodles. Spread with the remaining tomato sauce. Sprinkle generously with the remaining ⅓ cup (75 mL) grated Parmesan.

Bake for 40 minutes in the center of the oven, or until the lasagna is bubbling and the cheese topping is freckled. Pull out of the oven and let rest for 10 minutes before serving.

**PRESENTATION IS EVERYTHING**
Practical it may be, but the classic glass lasagna dish can grow dingy fast. Conceal its flaws with a same-sized wicker basket.

# Cobblestone Lasagna

SERVES 8

12 lasagna noodles
3 cups (750 mL) prepared pasta sauce (approx.)
2 recipes cooked meatballs (Spaghetti and Meatballs (page 40) or Cheatin' Italian Meatballs (page 44))
¾ lb (375 g) ricotta
½ lb (250 g) mozzarella, thinly sliced
1 cup (250 mL) grated Parmesan cheese

**FREEZING LASAGNA**
Because of the generous dimensions of these noodles and the fact that it's a certain amount of bother to make, lasagna recipes rarely feed less than eight. Wrap individual portions of leftovers in plastic wrap, then rewrap in foil. Unwrap and reheat in the microwave oven in a covered dish.

**ATLANTIC CITY'S MEATBALL-EATING CONTEST**
Winners are now close to downing 10 pounds at a time at the Tropicana World Meatball Eating Championship. A fact you could probably live without is that entrants are described as "gurgitators."

# Cheatin' Italian Meatballs • • •
# with Penne

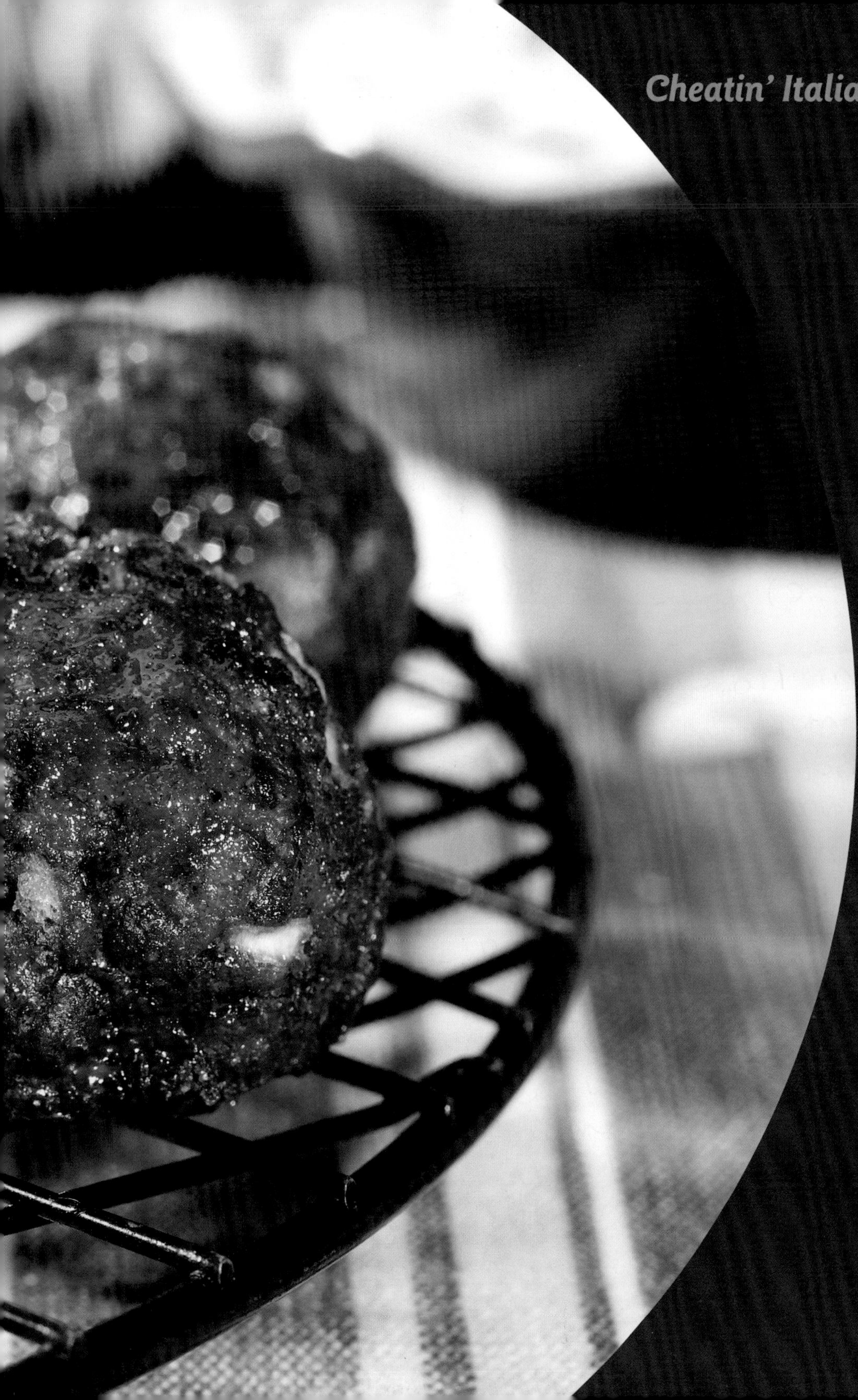

# Cheatin' Italian Meatballs with Penne

SERVES 4

1 lb (500 g) hot Italian sausage
2 tsp (10 mL) olive oil
one 28-oz (796-mL) can
    crushed tomatoes
1 Tbsp (15 mL) dried basil
¼ tsp (1 mL) dried chili flakes,
    or to taste (optional)
1 lb (500 g) penne or other
    chunky pasta, cooked
2 Tbsp (30 mL) chopped
    parsley

**SUPER EASY SEASONED MEATBALLS**
It was a light-bulb-going-on moment when I realized that all those scrumptious gourmet sausages—lamb with mint and oregano, beef with basil and sun-dried tomatoes—were simply already seasoned meatballs waiting to happen. Squeeze them out of their skins, shape the mixture into balls, and continue on from there.

*I've been making this dish for years because it's tasty, foolproof, and everyone likes it. While the recipe specifies hot Italian sausage, any well-seasoned variety works. See what your local sausage-iste can provide. If you're stuck for time, simply slice the sausages into ¾-inch (2-cm) lengths and hurl them into the pan. In all fairness, I should warn you that, while they'll still taste good, their skins shrink as they cook, making them look like fat little corset-constricted midriffs.*

Squeeze the sausage meat out of the skins. Dampen your hands and shape the meat mixture into 1-inch (2.5-cm) meatballs.

Heat the oil in a skillet over medium heat. Brown the meatballs on all sides, about 7 to 10 minutes. Scoop them out and drain on paper towels. Discard the fat in the skillet.

Return the meatballs to the skillet along with the tomatoes, basil, and chili flakes (if using). Bring to a boil, reduce the heat to low, and simmer, covered, for 20 minutes or until the meatballs are cooked through. Remove the lid and simmer 5 minutes longer to thicken the sauce.

Serve over the pasta. Sprinkle with the chopped parsley.

**PRESENTATION IS EVERYTHING**
If you have an old cast iron skillet, use it and bring it unashamedly to the table straight from la cucina.

*Hearty stews normally call for long leisurely cooking. This is the quick version. The idea is that you cook the meatballs Sunday morning, let the vegetable base mellow in the oven while you go out for a brisk but short walk, and combine everything when you get in the door. Serve with a big loaf of warmed, crisp-crusted bread or buttery mashed potatoes. While most stews taste better made in advance, this is at its best the day you make it.*

Preheat the oven to 350°F (180°C).

Heat the butter and oil in a large ovenproof saucepan over medium heat. Add the onions and garlic, and cook until softened, about 7 to 10 minutes. Add the carrots and celery, and continue cooking, stirring occasionally, until the vegetables are slightly softened and gilded with butter, about 5 minutes longer. Add the flour and stir well, making sure that it's thoroughly mixed in. Reduce the heat to low and cook for a further 3 to 4 minutes.

Pour in the beef stock. Add the herbs. Bring to a boil, and reduce so that the mixture is just simmering. Cover and place in the center of the oven for 40 minutes. Add the mushrooms and meatballs, and cook for 20 minutes longer or until the mushrooms are cooked and the meatballs heated through. Season to taste.

Sprinkle with the parsley before serving.

**PRESENTATION IS EVERYTHING**
Skip the parsley and place a sprig of fresh thyme on the top of the stew.

# Sunday Afternoon Meatball Stew

SERVES 4

1 Tbsp (15 mL) butter
1 Tbsp (15 mL) olive oil
⅔ cup (150 mL) coarsely chopped onions
½ tsp (2 mL) finely chopped garlic
1 cup (250 mL) carrots, cut in 1-inch (2.5-cm) chunks
⅔ cup (150 mL) sliced celery
1 Tbsp (15 mL) flour
4 cups (1 L) beef stock
1 tsp (5 mL) thyme
1 bay leaf
⅔ cup (150 mL) quartered mushrooms
1 recipe cooked meatballs (see sidebar)
salt and pepper to taste
chopped parsley to garnish

**MEATBALLS THAT LIKE GETTING STEWED**
For this dish, you need something fairly traditional—like the meatballs in Spaghetti and Meatballs (page 40), Ragoût de Boulettes (page 98), or Boules Bourguignon (page 122).

# Balls with an Edge

SERVES 4

1 lb (500 g) ground lamb
1 egg, slightly beaten
¼ cup (60 mL) finely chopped
   onions
2 Tbsp (30 mL) chopped fresh
   dill, or 2 tsp (10 mL) dried dill
1 tsp (5 mL) dried oregano
½ tsp (2 mL) finely chopped
   garlic
salt and pepper to taste
one 6-oz (170-mL) jar
   marinated artichoke hearts
2 Tbsp (30 mL) butter
2 Tbsp (30 mL) flour
2 cups (500 mL) chicken stock
2 Tbsp (30 mL) freshly
   squeezed lemon juice

*At the lunch we had to celebrate the start of this book, publisher Robert McCullough mentioned the possibility of square meatballs. I owe the name to him too. Edginess also comes in the sharp-flavored citric sauce. The trio of leading ingredients—lamb, artichokes, and lemon—was inspired by memories of a dinner in an Athens taverna.*

Preheat the oven to 425°F (220°C).

Mix together the ground lamb, egg, onions, dill, oregano, garlic, salt, and pepper. Gently pat into an 8-inch (20-cm) square non-stick pan. With a sharp knife, mark the meat mixture into 16 squares (each 2 inches/5 cm per side). Bake for 15 to 20 minutes or until the meat is cooked through.

Meanwhile, make the sauce. Drain the artichoke hearts, reserving the marinade. Chop them coarsely and set aside.

Melt the butter in a small saucepan; add the flour and whisk, stirring constantly, for 2 to 3 minutes. Pour in the chicken stock, and continue whisking until the sauce comes to a boil and thickens. Add the chopped artichoke hearts and the lemon juice. Taste and add more "edge" with the artichoke marinade.

Gently remove the meat squares from the baking dish, and place on individual plates or a platter. Drizzle the sauce over the top.

### PRESENTATION IS EVERYTHING

Dill-flecked rice is the prettiest accompaniment to this, or pita bread if you're strapped for time. To add a bright note of color, cook a batch of the Cheery Cherry Tomatoes on page 113.

*These herby, savory little morsels give you a bigger bang for your buck than most meatballs because of their rice content. Bolstering canned tomatoes with fresh peppers and mushrooms adds equal heft to the sauce. Little kids like these because of the "prickles." Serve with chunks of crusty bread.*

Combine the meat, rice, onion, egg, herbs, salt, and pepper in a large bowl. Form into 1-inch (2.5-cm) meatballs. Set aside.

Heat the olive oil in a medium saucepan over medium heat. Add the chopped peppers, mushrooms, and zucchini and cook, stirring occasionally, for 5 minutes or until slightly softened. Add the tomatoes and bring to a boil. Reduce the heat and drop in the prepared meatballs one by one.

Simmer for 25 to 30 minutes, or until the meatballs have swollen and are cooked through.

**PRESENTATION IS EVERYTHING**
Flaunt the rainbow of colors in this dish by bringing it to the table in a wide but shallow pottery dish.

# Porcupine Meatballs

SERVES 4

1 lb (500 g) ground beef or lamb
½ cup (125 mL) rice
½ cup (125 mL) finely chopped onion
1 egg, slightly beaten
½ tsp (2 mL) dried thyme
½ tsp (2 mL) dried sage
salt and pepper to taste
1 Tbsp (15 mL) olive oil
1 cup (250 mL) coarsely chopped red or yellow peppers, or a mix (see sidebar)
½ cup (125 mL) coarsely chopped mushrooms
½ cup (125 mL) coarsely chopped zucchini
one 28-oz (796-mL) can tomatoes with juice, coarsely chopped

**CHEAP PEPPER TRICK**
If a recipe calls for chopped peppers, of whatever color, buy the slightly dented or damaged ones that produce stores often sell by the bag for one-half or less of the usual price.

# Great Balls of Fire

SERVES 4

1 lb (500 g) ground pork
½ cup (125 mL) finely chopped
   onion
1 egg, slightly beaten
½ tsp (2 mL) finely chopped
   garlic
½ tsp (2 mL) minced jalapeño
   pepper, or to taste
cayenne pepper to taste
½ tsp (2 mL) dried chili flakes,
   or to taste
1 Tbsp (15 mL) chili powder
1 tsp (5 mL) cumin seeds,
   ground
1 Tbsp (15 mL) olive oil
one 9-oz (540-mL) can black
   beans, drained and rinsed
one 28-oz (796-mL) can
   tomatoes, chopped
whole dried chilies (optional)

*Chili sauces, jalapeño peppers, cayenne used with a lavish hand . . . in the past couple of decades we've acquired a tolerance for spice that would have made earlier generations swoon. With their triple hit of powdered, flaked, and fresh chilies, these are potentially meatballs from hell. To counteract internal flames caused by this one-pot supper, serve an antidote alongside—such as cooling mango or nectarine salsa, or a salad of avocados, apples (or oranges), and watercress.*

Combine the ground pork, onion, egg, garlic, and spices in a large bowl. Mix together gently but thoroughly to distribute the "heat" evenly. Shape into 1-inch (2.5-cm) balls. Be sure to wear disposable rubber gloves or wash your hands afterwards.

Heat the olive oil in a non-stick skillet. Cook the meatballs for 15 minutes, or until browned and almost cooked through. Drain on paper towels and discard the fat in the pan.

Return the meatballs to the pan. Mix the black beans and tomatoes together in a bowl, and pour over and around the meatballs. Add the whole dried chilies if you are using them (brave you!). Bring to a boil, and simmer uncovered until the sauce is throbbing and the meatballs are cooked through.

### PRESENTATION IS EVERYTHING
Nothing succeeds like excess . . . scatter fine rings of hot red pepper over the dish. This is no time to be shy. Otherwise, a few sprigs of cilantro.

# Boulettes de Veau

SERVES 4

*I clipped this recipe out of a southern French newspaper and fiddled around with it. If you can't find ground veal, beef works well too. This is how the French interpret a cheese and bacon burger, except that it's infinitely better. Small pieces of bacon called "lardons" are so prevalent in French country cooking that even the supermarkets sell them already pre-cut.*

½ cup (125 mL) finely chopped bacon (about 2 slices)
¾ cup (175 mL) finely chopped onion
1 lb (500 g) ground veal or lean ground beef
1 cup (250 mL) fine dry breadcrumbs
⅔ cup (150 mL) grated Parmesan cheese
1 egg, slightly beaten
1 tsp (5 mL) dried thyme
1 tsp (5 mL) dried oregano
1 tsp (5 mL) dried basil
1 tsp (5 mL) finely chopped garlic
salt and pepper to taste
⅓ cup (75 mL) beef stock
⅓ cup (75 mL) red or white wine
2 Tbsp (30 mL) finely chopped parsley

Cook the bacon in a large skillet over low heat until transparent but not crisp, about 10 minutes. Set aside.

Add the onion to the bacon fat in the skillet and cook until softened, about 5 minutes. Scoop out the onion with a slotted spoon.

Mix the cooked bacon with the cooked onions, ground veal, breadcrumbs, cheese, egg, herbs, salt, and pepper in a large bowl. Form into balls 1 inch (2.5 cm) in diameter. In the skillet, brown the meatballs in the bacon fat over medium-high heat until crusty on the outside, about 10 minutes. Turn them gently as they are quite delicate. Drain on a paper towel and discard any fat in the pan.

Return the meatballs to the pan, and pour in the beef stock and wine. Reduce the heat and simmer for 15 to 20 minutes. Sprinkle with the parsley.

Serve the meatballs with noodles or rice.

**PRESENTATION IS EVERYTHING**
Old blue-and-white plates from France would be the choice in the best of all possible worlds. Retro '70s brown pottery bowls found at a yard sale also have the right Gallic spirit.

# Turkey Balls with Cardamom, Lemon, and Cream

SERVES 4

1 lb (500 g) ground turkey
½ cup (125 mL) fresh white
   breadcrumbs
¼ cup (60 mL) finely chopped
   green onions
2 tsp (10 mL) grated lemon rind
seeds from 8 green cardamom
   pods, finely ground, or ½ tsp
   (2 mL) ground cardamom
1 egg, slightly beaten
1 pinch of cayenne pepper
salt to taste
1 Tbsp (15 mL) vegetable oil
½ cup (125 mL) sour cream or
   crème fraîche (see sidebar)
¼ cup (125 mL) turkey or
   chicken stock
1 Tbsp (15 mL) lemon juice
2 Tbsp (30 mL) finely chopped
   parsley
salt and pepper to taste

*Ground turkey, in fact turkey in general, doesn't show up on tables as frequently as it could, so I've used it here, seasoning it with the clean, pungent flavor of cardamom and adding lemon rind for even more sparkle. Serve these with egg noodles or, given the Indian spicing, basmati rice spritzed with lemon juice.*

Combine the ground turkey, breadcrumbs, green onions, lemon rind, cardamom, egg, cayenne pepper, and salt in a bowl. Dampen your hands and shape the mixture into 1-inch (2.5-cm) balls.

Heat the oil over medium-low in a skillet, add the meatballs, and cook for 12 to 15 minutes, rolling them around in the pan so that they brown evenly. Place in a warmed serving dish, cover with foil, and keep warm.

Over low heat, whisk together the sour cream, stock, and lemon juice in a small saucepan. Bring to the boil, stir in 1 Tbsp (15 mL) of the parsley, and simmer until slightly thickened. Season to taste. Pour over turkey balls and sprinkle with the remaining parsley.

### PRESENTATION IS EVERYTHING

This is a pale dish, so better use that parsley or the style police will get you. If you're serving rice, try the red variety or a multicolored mix.

### HOW TO MAKE CRÈME FRAÎCHE

If you can't get your hands on real crème fraîche, it's easy to make your own. Whisk 1 cup (250 mL) whipping cream until very slightly thickened. Fold in 1 Tbsp (15 mL) buttermilk. Mix the two together in a large bowl, and pour into a lidded glass jar (a clean, empty, pasta sauce jar is ideal). Shake well and leave on the kitchen counter until thickened, usually a day or two (it depends on the time of year and the temperature of your kitchen). When it's thickened, put the jar in the fridge. Refrigerated, crème fraîche will keep 7 to 10 days. It gets tangier as it ages. You'll find it invaluable for spooning over fresh fruit or for smoothing sauces.

# Lamb and Anchovy Meatballs with Cream Sauce

**SERVES 4**

1½ cups (375 mL) fresh
    breadcrumbs
1 cup (250 mL) milk
1 lb (500 g) ground lamb
one 2-oz (50-g) can of anchovy
    fillets, drained, oil reserved
1 tsp (5 mL) chopped garlic
⅓ cup (75 mL) finely chopped
    parsley
salt and pepper to taste
¼ cup (60 mL) flour (approx.)
1 Tbsp (15 mL) vegetable oil
½ cup (125 mL) sour cream or
    crème fraîche (see page 50)
2 Tbsp (30 mL) chicken stock

*The surprise here is that the anchovies don't taste at all fishy, but they do add levels of flavor to an otherwise simple dish. This sunny Mediterranean combination teams well with a green salad, or sliced tomatoes dotted with black olives, or pan-fried red and green peppers (see recipe on page 53)—with, in all cases, wedges torn off a loaf of country bread.*

Pour the milk over the breadcrumbs, let soak for 5 minutes, drain off any excess milk and mash into a paste. Place in a large bowl, and add the ground lamb and oil from the anchovies.

Whiz the anchovies and garlic together in a food processor into a paste. Add to the meat mixture, and mix well so that the anchovy and garlic paste is evenly distributed. Add the parsley (reserving 2 Tbsp/ 30 mL for garnish), and season to taste (bearing in mind that anchovies are pretty salty).

Moisten your hands and make 1-inch (2.5-cm) meatballs. Roll them in the flour.

Heat the oil in a non-stick skillet over medium-low heat, and cook the meatballs for 20 minutes, rolling them around so they turn golden all over and are cooked through. Set aside and keep warm.

Meanwhile, gently warm the sour cream and chicken stock in a small saucepan. Season to taste with more salt and pepper. Pour over the meatballs, sprinkle with the remaining parsley, and serve.

**PRESENTATION IS EVERYTHING**
Forget the parsley this time around and sprinkle on a little paprika.

*The moment the barbecue season begins, health authorities start banging on about how we should cook ground beef all the way through. Ah yes, there's nothing like a good, dry burger. One way inventive chefs get around this is by hiding a chunk of cheese in the patty. As it cooks, the cheese melts, keeping the burger moist and adding savory flavor. Works for meatballs too.*

Combine everything—except the cheese and oil—in a bowl. Shape the meat mixture around the cheese cubes to form 1-inch (2.5-cm) meatballs.

Heat the oil in a skillet over medium heat. Add the meatballs and cook for 15 minutes, rolling them around so that they cook evenly and the centers are molten.

**PRESENTATION IS EVERYTHING**
Line them up in a sliced baguette with all the customary burger trimmings. Works for me.

## Mediterranean Peppers   SERVES 4

1 Tbsp (15 mL) olive oil
1 cup (250 mL) thinly sliced red peppers
1 cup (250 mL) thinly sliced yellow peppers
½ cup (125 mL) small black olives, pitted

Heat the oil in a skillet over medium heat. Add the peppers and toss to coat with the oil. Reduce the heat to medium-low and continue cooking until the peppers are tender-crisp, about 10 minutes. Add the olives, and cook for a further 3 minutes or until the olives are heated through.

# Molten Meatballs

SERVES 4

1 lb (500 g) ground beef
⅓ cup (75 mL) finely chopped onion
1 Tbsp (15 mL) tomato paste
1½ tsp (7 mL) dried oregano
1 tsp (5 mL) finely minced garlic
salt and pepper to taste
6 oz (175 g) cheddar or Emmenthal cheese, cut in ½-inch (1-cm) cubes
1 Tbsp (15 mL) vegetable oil

**. . . AND WILL YOU HAVE FRIES WITH THAT?**
These meatballs don't have a sauce, so you want a "goopy" vegetable alongside for moisture. Onions, thinly sliced and cooked slowly until they melt into a soft brown mass, are one option and in line with the hamburger inspiration behind this recipe. So is a salad of shredded iceberg lettuce, sliced red onion, tomato. For Oven-Fries, see page 65.

54 Balls!

# Sweet and Sour Meatballs

SERVES 4

1 lb (500 g) ground pork
⅓ cup (75 mL) coarsely
   chopped walnuts
⅓ cup (75 mL) finely chopped
   cilantro
⅓ cup (75 mL) finely chopped
   green onions
1 Tbsp (15 mL) ketchup
5 tsp (25 mL) soy sauce
2 tsp (10 mL) finely chopped
   fresh ginger
1 tsp (5 mL) finely chopped
   garlic
¼ tsp (1 mL) dried chili flakes
1 Tbsp (15 mL) vegetable oil
½ cup (125 mL) water or
   chicken stock
2 Tbsp (30 mL) hoisin sauce
1 Tbsp (15 mL) cornstarch
1 Tbsp (15 mL) rice or wine
   vinegar

*The term "sweet and sour" conjures up soggy, battered chunks of meat in a glue-y, neon-colored sauce. Forget all that. For a start, the sauce is only slightly sweet from its hoisin content, and walnuts provide appetizing crunch. Rice is the obvious go-with, along with steamed or stir-fried carrots, snowpeas, or broccoli drizzled with sesame oil and sprinkled with toasted sesame seeds.*

Mix together the ground pork, walnuts, ¼ cup (60 mL) each of the cilantro and the green onions, the ketchup, 2 tsp (10 mL) of the soy sauce, the ginger, garlic, and chili flakes. Dampen your hands and shape the mixture into 1-inch (2.5-cm) meatballs. Chill for 2 hours.

Heat the oil in a large skillet over medium heat and add the meatballs. Reduce the heat to medium-low, and cook the meatballs for about 20 minutes until they are browned all over. Transfer to a dish lined with paper towels and keep warm.

Empty the fat out of the pan, and add the water or chicken stock, hoisin sauce, cornstarch, vinegar, and remaining soy sauce over low heat. Raise the heat until the sauce comes to a boil and thickens. Spoon over the meatballs, and sprinkle with the remaining cilantro and green onions.

### PRESENTATION IS EVERYTHING
Imagine these meatballs in a deep green, lacquered serving bowl from Chinatown.

*Real shepherd's pie is made with the remains of the Sunday lamb roast. If beef is used, it's called cottage pie. Normally, traditional shepherd's pie has a disconcerting habit of collapsing in a large brown and beige puddle when you dish it onto a plate. This approach makes for a more polite-looking presentation. Serve with butter-gilded carrots or peas or steamed broccoli.*

1 lb (500 g) ground lamb
¼ cup (60 mL) chopped onion
1 tsp (5 mL) dried thyme
1 bay leaf, crumbled
salt and pepper to taste
1 dash of Worcestershire sauce, or to taste
2 Tbsp (30 mL) oil
⅓ cup (75 mL) butter
1 Tbsp (15 mL) flour
1 cup (250 mL) beef stock or broth
3 large potatoes, peeled and cut into 1-inch (2.5-cm) slices
¼ cup (60 mL) warmed milk

Preheat the oven to 375°F (190°C).

Combine the ground lamb, onion, dried thyme, and bay leaf in a bowl. Season to taste with salt, pepper, and Worcestershire sauce. Form into 1-inch (2.5-cm) balls. Heat the oil in a skillet over medium-high and brown the meatballs (you don't have to cook them through as they will finish cooking in the oven). Transfer the meatballs to a 6-cup (1.5-L) ovenproof casserole dish.

Meanwhile, heat 1 Tbsp (15 mL) of the butter in a saucepan over medium heat. Add the flour and whisk until smooth. Pour in the beef stock and bring to a boil. Reduce and simmer until the sauce thickens. Season to taste. Remove from the heat, pour the "gravy" over the meatballs, and set aside.

Cook the potatoes in simmering water for 15 minutes or until tender. Drain, and mash with 3 Tbsp (45 mL) more of the butter and the milk to a smooth purée. Season to taste.

Spread the potatoes over the meatballs and gravy, dot with the remaining butter, and place in the oven for 30 minutes or until the gravy is bubbling, the meatballs are cooked through, and the top is browned and crisp.

**PRESENTATION IS EVERYTHING**

If you own little ovenproof ramekins, making individual shepherd's pies is the work of a moment.

# ...on a Roll

1 lb (500 g) ground lean beef
1 egg, slightly beaten
¼ cup (60 mL) fresh white
   breadcrumbs
½ tsp (2 mL) finely chopped
   garlic
1 tsp (5 mL) Dijon mustard, or
   to taste
cayenne pepper to taste
dried chili peppers to taste
salt and pepper to taste
1 Tbsp (15 mL) olive oil
one 14-oz (398-mL) can of
   tomatoes
hot sauce to taste
2 baguettes, each halved, or
   4 mini-baguettes
2 cups shredded iceberg lettuce

*If your only experience of the meatball sub is the takeout variety, taste the difference when you make it from scratch. Here, a basic meat mix gets oomph from cayenne, chilies, and mustard. By all means make the meatballs ahead of time, but don't assemble the sandwiches until just before serving or the bread will be soggy.*

Combine the ground beef, egg, breadcrumbs, garlic, Dijon mustard, cayenne, and dried chili peppers and in a large bowl. Season to taste and shape into 1-inch (2.5-cm) meatballs.

Heat the olive oil in a skillet, and cook the meatballs over medium heat, turning until they are browned on all sides and cooked through (15 to 20 minutes).

Meanwhile, tip the tomatoes into a saucepan, chop roughly, and bring to a boil over medium heat. Reduce the heat and let simmer until thickened. Add hot sauce to taste.

Split the bread; add the lettuce, the cooked meatballs, and a spoonful or two of the thickened tomato sauce. You can freeze the leftover sauce until next time.

### PRESENTATION IS EVERYTHING

This dish isn't about looks, it's about flavor. Be generous with the paper napkins and don't wear anything that calls for dry cleaning.

# Chicken "Balls" and Dumplings

SERVES 4

"Balls" is in quotes because these are actually chunks of juicy chicken. Nourishing, tasty—this is comfort food at its best. Kids like it because of the "nuggets" and the corn. Parents like it because the addition of dumplings means they don't have to mess around with rice or potatoes. You need a skillet or pot with a lid for this—dumplings, like mushrooms, only reach their full potential in damp darkness.

Heat the oil in a skillet or pot over medium heat, and brown the chicken chunks on all side, about 7 minutes. Add the onions and carrots, lower the heat, and continue to cook for 5 minutes, stirring often. Add the corn and thyme, and season. Pour in the chicken stock, cover, and simmer for 20 minutes.

While the chicken cooks, prepare the dumplings. Combine the flour, milk, egg, baking powder, and salt in a bowl and mix roughly (the mixture doesn't have to be smooth). Spoon the batter in 1-Tbsp (15-mL) dollops on top of the chicken, leaving space between them for the dumplings to swell. Put on the lid, return the skillet or pot to the stove, and continue simmering for 10 to 12 minutes until the dumplings puff up.

**PRESENTATION IS EVERYTHING**
Dish this out into deep bowls so it stays warm till the last spoonful.

1 Tbsp (15 mL) vegetable oil
1½ lb (750 g) boneless, skinless chicken thighs, cut in 1½-inch (4-cm) chunks
1 cup (250 mL) coarsely chopped onions
¾ cup (175 mL) thickly sliced carrots
one 19-oz (540-mL) can of corn
1 tsp (5 mL) dried thyme
salt and pepper to taste
1½ cups (375 mL) chicken stock
1 cup (250 mL) flour
½ cup (125 mL) milk
1 egg
2 tsp (10 mL) baking powder
½ tsp (2 mL) salt

**MAZATLAN STYLE**
Incorporate dried chilies and oregano instead of thyme, and you're on your way to a Mexican variation.

# Fish Balls

# Albondigas de Pescado
# (Fish Balls in Tomato Sauce)

SERVES 4

2 Tbsp (30 mL) olive oil
¼ cup (60 mL) finely chopped onion
1 Tbsp (15 mL) finely chopped garlic
one 19-oz (540-mL) can tomatoes with juice, coarsely chopped
3 Tbsp (45 mL) chopped parsley
1 tsp (5 mL) dried thyme
¼ cup (60 mL) fresh white breadcrumbs
2 Tbsp (30 mL) white vinegar
1½ lb (750 g) cod, or other mild-flavored firm white fish
1 cup (250 mL) chopped tomatoes, canned or fresh
2 eggs, beaten
2 Tbsp (30 mL) finely chopped parsley
2 tsp (10 mL) finely chopped onion
½ tsp (2 mL) finely chopped garlic
1 chili poblano, canned, cut into strips
¼ cup (60 mL) coarsely chopped black olives

*Like a lot of recipes for round food, the original starting point for albondigas was probably leftovers. Leftover fish, in this case. Little scraps scraped off the carcass. Tender nuggets from behind the ears. Popular along the Mexican coast, albondigas are delicious with rice or warmed tortillas, and a cucumber salad.*

Make the sauce first. Heat the olive oil in a large saucepan over medium heat, and add the onion and garlic. Cook, stirring continuously, until golden. Add the tomatoes, parsley, and thyme. Continue cooking until the sauce thickens slightly. Set aside and keep warm.

Place the breadcrumbs in a bowl and sprinkle with the vinegar.

Cut the fish into 1-inch (2.5-cm) pieces, and pulse in a food processor until finely chopped (no further, you don't want a paste). Combine the moistened bread, chopped fish, tomatoes, eggs, 1 Tbsp (15 mL) of the parsley, the onion, and the garlic. Make into balls 1½ inches (4 cm) in diameter.

Bring the tomato sauce to a simmer. Add the fish balls and cook gently for 15 to 20 minutes. Using a slotted spoon, remove the fish balls to a warmed platter and cover them loosely with foil. Add the chili poblano strips and the olives to the tomato sauce. Cook for 2 to 3 minutes longer so the flavors can get to know each other. Pour the sauce over the fishballs. Sprinkle with the remaining parsley.

PRESENTATION IS EVERYTHING

As with other Mexican dishes in this book, this is a rare opportunity to actually use those horrendously bright tablemats and that clunky souvenir pottery you bought in the mercado.

*Why do I think mai tais would make good pre-dinner drinks? Probably because this dish has a retro Polynesian feel to it. Serve these tender morsels with rice and lightly steamed Chinese greens. Look for small or medium-sized shrimp. You'll be chopping them up anyway so there's little point in buying big expensive ones.*

# Shrimp Balls in Coconut and Pineapple Sauce

SERVES 4

1 lb (500 g) shelled, deveined shrimp, finely chopped
2 Tbsp (30 mL) coarsely chopped water chestnuts
1 egg white
2 Tbsp (30 mL) plus 1 tsp (5mL) vegetable oil
1 Tbsp (15 mL) finely chopped fresh ginger
1 Tbsp (15 mL) finely chopped green onion
1 Tbsp (15 mL) white wine or water
½ tsp (2 mL) cornstarch
1 tsp (5 mL) finely chopped garlic
1 cup (250 mL) coconut milk
½ cup (125 mL) pineapple juice
1 tsp (5 mL) soy sauce
lemon wedges to garnish
cilantro sprigs to garnish

Combine the shrimp, water chestnuts, egg white, 1 tsp (5 mL) of the vegetable oil, ginger, onion, wine, and cornstarch in a bowl and mix well. Shape into 1-inch (2.5-cm) balls.

Heat 1 Tbsp (15 mL) of the vegetable oil in a non-stick skillet, and fry the shrimp balls on all sides until golden and cooked through, about 10 minutes. Set aside on a warmed platter. Tent with foil.

Meanwhile, in a saucepan, heat the remaining 1 Tbsp (15 mL) of the vegetable oil over medium heat, add the garlic, and cook for 5 minutes. Add the coconut milk, pineapple juice, and soy sauce, bring to a boil, and simmer until slightly thickened.

Pour the sauce over the shrimp balls, garnish with the lemon wedges and cilantro, and serve immediately.

**PRESENTATION IS EVERYTHING**
Bring out your tiki mugs and those coconut shell bowls you had earmarked for your next yard sale. Tell your friends to wear their most horrendously patterned Hawaiian shirts.

# Far Eastern Fish Ball Chowder

SERVES 4

¼ cup (60 mL) chopped bacon
½ cup (125 mL) coarsely
  chopped onion
½ cup (125 mL) coarsely
  chopped celery
2 cups (500 mL) water
2 cups (500 mL) diced potatoes
1 lb (500 g) Asian fish balls (see
  sidebar), or salmon (or cod)
  fillet cut into 1-inch (2.5-cm)
  chunks
2 cups (500 mL) whole milk
2 tsp (10 mL) soy sauce
¼ cup (60 mL) chopped cilantro
1 tsp (5 mL) sesame oil

**FISH BALLS TO GO**
Asian supermarkets often sell
fresh or frozen fish balls made
of seasoned fish paste (the fish
is usually pollock or hake). The
consistency is much smoother
than Western fish balls, and
they can seem rubbery the first
time you taste them cooked.
After that, you become addicted.
Throw a few purchased fish balls
into chicken broth with chopped
Chinese greens and rice noodles.
Top with chopped green onion,
and drizzle with soy sauce and
sesame oil. Now, that's a fast
supper.

*Oddly, Newfoundland-meets-Cantonese fusion cuisine has never made it into trendy restaurants. I'm not convinced that it ever will, but this mix of ingredients—part from Canada's far east, part from what Brits used to call "the Far East"—might launch a trend. Fish chowder is wonderfully warming on a chilly winter's night. Cheap, easy, tasty. With potatoes already inside it, you don't even need bread. A true one-bowl meal.*

Cook the bacon in a large saucepan over medium heat until crisp. Remove the bacon bits with a slotted spoon and set aside. Add the onion and celery to the bacon fat, and cook until slightly softened, about 5 minutes.

Add the water and the potatoes. Bring to a boil. Cover, reduce the heat, and simmer for 10 minutes. Add the fish and cook 5 to 7 minutes longer. Add the milk and soy sauce, and heat gently until barely simmering. Serve sprinkled with the chopped cilantro and drizzled with the sesame oil.

### PRESENTATION IS EVERYTHING

All Chinatowns sell wonderful lidded soup tureens, usually white ones with blue fish painted on them. Beat that for appropriateness. While you're shopping, buy four small matching bowls too.

# Sushi Style Shrimp Ball Salad

SERVES 4

¾ cup (175 mL) sushi rice
¾ cup (175 mL) water
3 Tbsp (45 mL) rice wine
  vinegar
1 tsp (5 mL) sugar
6 oz (175 g) small shrimp,
  coarsely chopped
½ cup (125 mL) finely diced
  cucumber
½ cup (125 mL) finely diced
  carrot
¼ cup (60 mL) thinly sliced
  green onion
¼ cup (60 mL) Japanese or
  regular mayonnaise
2 tsp (10 mL) soy sauce
½ tsp (2 mL) wasabi
1 sheet of nori (dried seaweed),
  cut into very small squares
  (use scissors)
4 cups (1 L) washed salad
  greens
¾ cup (175 mL) cubed ripe
  avocado
2 Tbsp (30 mL) finely shredded
  pickled ginger
3 Tbsp (45 mL) olive oil
¼ cup (60 mL) toasted sesame
  seeds

*Making genuine sushi from scratch takes time, which is why I like Toronto cookbook writer Rose Reisman's idea of a sushi salad. My version uses shrimp, and adds avocado and peach-pink pickled ginger to the greens. Chop the vegetables while the rice is cooking and cooling, and you can whip this up in 30 minutes.*

Bring the rice and water to a boil over medium heat. Lower the heat, cover, and cook for 15 minutes. Stir in 2 Tbsp (30 mL) of the rice wine vinegar and the sugar, and let cool to room temperature. Stir in the shrimp, cucumber, carrot, green onion, mayonnaise, soy sauce, wasabi, and nori.

Combine the greens, avocado, and pickled ginger in a large bowl. In a smaller bowl, whisk together the remaining rice wine vinegar and the olive oil. Toss the salad with the dressing, and place on 4 plates.

Using an ice cream scoop, make 3 sushi balls to place on top of each salad. Sprinkle with the sesame seeds.

**PRESENTATION IS EVERYTHING**
Bring out your square or oblong sushi plates.

**OPEN SESAME (SEEDS)**
Besides contributing crunch to this salad, toasted sesame seeds are handy to keep on hand for sprinkling over salads, stir fries, yogurt, or breakfast cereal. Heat a non-stick skillet over medium heat. Cover the bottom of the pan with a one-seed-deep layer of unhulled sesame seeds. Cook carefully, stirring and tossing, until they turn evenly brown all over. Store in a lidded jar in the fridge.

*I'm not a fan of deep-frying. All that spluttering, all those spatters. So these fish "balls" are coated with panko crumbs for crispness and popped in the oven. The "chips" cook at the same time. Serve with mushy peas, which are simply frozen peas cooked as the packet tells you, then whizzed in a food processor until smooth as suede. You can make the peas ahead of time—reheat them gently as dinner time approaches, with a little whipping cream whisked in if the mixture is too thick.*

# Crunchy Fish Balls and Oven-Fried Chips

SERVES 4

4 large baking potatoes,
   unpeeled
¼ cup (60 mL) vegetable oil
salt and pepper to taste
1 lb (500 g) firm white fish, cut
   into 1½-inch (4-cm) chunks
1 egg, slightly beaten
½ cup (125 mL) panko crumbs

Preheat the oven to 375°F (190°C).

Cut each potato lengthwise into 8 wedges. Mix the oil, salt, and pepper together in a plastic bag. Add the potatoes, and scrumple them around until they are evenly coated with oil and seasonings.

Tumble onto a rimmed baking sheet, and place in the oven on the center shelf. Cook for 20 minutes.

Meanwhile, prepare the fish. Using 2 spoons, dip each piece of fish into the beaten egg and then into the panko crumbs so they are evenly coated.

When the potatoes have cooked for 20 minutes, turn them, push them to one side of the baking sheet, and place the fish "balls" alongside. Continue cooking for 20 minutes (turning the fish after 10 minutes), or until the fish and chips are crisp and cooked through.

PRESENTATION IS EVERYTHING

I'd say serve the fish and chips in newspaper for true authenticity (what English person of a certain age didn't learn everything they needed to know about sex from reading grease-spotted pages of *The News of the World*). But even in Britain, they don't do that any more. And "set them in a polystyrene clamshell" just doesn't have the same ring. Plain white plates and an unadorned bottle of malt vinegar on the table. Lemon wedges are ever so posh.

**PANKO CRUMBS**
Panko are Japanese bread crumbs that deliver a crunchier coating than the usual kind. Asian grocery stores usually carry them.

# Marseillaise Ball-abaisse

**SERVES 8**

3 Tbsp (45 mL) olive oil
2 cups (500 mL) coarsely
    chopped onions
8 cups fish stock or water (see
    sidebar)
1 bottle dry white wine
2 cups (500 mL) coarsely
    chopped tomatoes (fresh, or
    canned and drained)
1 cup (250 mL) coarsely
    chopped fennel
⅓ cup (75 mL) chopped parsley
1 Tbsp (15 mL) finely chopped
    garlic
2 tsp (10 mL) fennel seeds
2 tsp (10 mL) dried thyme
1 large pinch of saffron
1 strip of fresh orange rind,
    about ½ inch (1 cm) wide and
    3 inches (8 cm) long
2 lb (1 kg) Asian fish balls, or
    white fish cut into 1-inch
    (2.5-cm) chunks
2 lb (1 kg) mussels or clams
2 lb (1 kg) medium-sized
    shrimp, peeled and deveined
salt and pepper to taste
1 baguette, cut into ½-inch
    (1-cm) slices, toasted both
    sides (see sidebar)
1 fat garlic clove, halved
rouille (see sidebar)

*No prizes for guessing that this is a down-market (translation, affordable) adaptation of the classic southern French soup. If you feel that leaving lobster out is culinary slumming, bear in mind that authentic bouillabaisse, as served in Marseille, was originally merely a means of using up odds and ends of the day's catch. This looks like a huge production but it's actually not. You can make the soup base (and the rouille) in the morning, or even the day before, then add the fish minutes before serving.*

Heat the oil in a large pot over medium heat, add the onions, and cook, stirring frequently until softened and golden, about 15 minutes. Add the stock, wine, tomatoes, herbs, and orange rind. Bring to a boil, reduce the heat until the mixture is just simmering, cover, and cook for 45 minutes. Refrigerate if not using immediately.

Bring the soup to a boil, uncovered. Add the fish balls and mussels, and cook for 5 minutes. Add the shrimp and cook for 3 minutes more, or until the shellfish have opened and the shrimp have turned pink. Taste and adjust the seasoning with the salt and pepper.

While the fish is cooking, smear the toasted baguette slices with garlic and place in a napkin-lined basket. Serve the rouille in a bowl on the side for people to add at will.

### PRESENTATION IS EVERYTHING
Edith Piaf playing, candles in wine bottles, checked napkins . . . that should whisk everyone to a French harbor, if only in their imaginations.

## FISH STOCK

Bouillabaisse recipes often suggest asking your fish person for bones and trimmings. Good luck. What I do is freeze shrimp shells as they come my way, then simmer them in water to extract their goodness. Simply strain the resultant broth and freeze until needed. If you can get your hands on lobster or crab shells, do the same. Also worth saving are the juices from cooked mussels or clams (taste to see that they're not too salty). In all cases, strain once cooked and freeze immediately.

## ROUILLE (RUSTY MAYONNAISE)

Red and fiery, rouille (French for "rust") is the thick glossy mayonnaise-like sauce served with fish soups in the south along the Mediterranean coast (it's so common, you can even buy it by the jar in French supermarkets). Some recipes stipulate breadcrumbs. The easy one calls for 1 cup (250 mL) Hellmann's mayonnaise, and finely chopped garlic and cayenne pepper to taste: start with 1 tsp (5 mL) of garlic and ½ tsp (2 mL) of cayenne, and go up from there.

## MAKING BAGUETTE TOASTS

You can toast baguette slices under the broiler of course, but it's less effort to arrange them in a non-stick skillet over medium-high heat. Either way you need to keep an eye on them, as they go from golden brown to charcoal black in the time it takes the setting sun to drop into the Mediterranean.

## TOMATOES IN SEASON

In summer, use lovely ripe fresh tomatoes. In winter, they've probably traveled for thousands of miles so give them a miss; for flavor and color, go with the canned variety.

# San Francisco Seafood Stew and Sourdough Boules

SERVES 8

3 Tbsp (45 mL) olive oil
¾ cup (175 mL) coarsely
 chopped onion
one 28-oz (796-mL) can of
 tomatoes, chopped
one 19-oz (540-mL) can of
 tomato sauce
2 cups (500 mL) fish stock or
 water
1 cup (250 mL) chopped green
 pepper
1 cup (250 mL) dry white wine
¾ cup (175 mL) chopped
 parsley
2 tsp (10 mL) dried basil
1 tsp (5 mL) dried oregano
1 tsp (5 mL) chopped garlic
1 bay leaf
2 lb (1 kg) clams or mussels
1½ lb (750 g) fish cut into 1-inch
 (2.5-cm) chunks, or Asian
 fish balls
1½ lb (750 g) large shrimp
salt and pepper to taste
1 large or 2 small sourdough
 boules

*The traditional sourdough "boule" is the "ball" element here. Originally from the U.S. west coast, this is one of those regional dishes that you come across in dozens of versions. Like bouillabaisse (or rather Ballabaisse) it probably evolved from what ingredients were around. As long as you keep the quantities more or less the same, feel free to substitute different fish and seafood.*

Heat the oil in a large pot over medium heat, add the onion, and cook until softened and golden, about 7 to 10 minutes. Add all the remaining ingredients, except for the seafood, salt and pepper, and boules. Bring to a boil, reduce the heat until the soup base is just simmering, cover, and cook for 45 minutes. Refrigerate if not using immediately.

Bring the soup to a boil, uncovered. Add the shellfish and fish, and cook for 5 minutes. Add the shrimp and cook for 3 minutes more, or until the shellfish have opened and the shrimp have turned pink. Taste and adjust the seasoning with the salt and pepper.

Ladle into wide soup plates, making sure that everyone gets a bit of everything. Serve with big chunks of the sourdough boules.

PRESENTATION IS EVERYTHING
Dishes like this are so handsome in their own right that they don't need garnishing, apart from lemon wedges on a separate little plate.

*Salmon is a miraculous fish. You can poach it, grill it, roast it, or barbecue it, and it's happy with just about any herb or spice. The ones in this dish add Indian nuances. Serve the salmon balls with basmati rice, and a raita (see page 86) of plain yogurt and chopped cucumber dusted with garam masala.*

Preheat the oven to 425°F (220°C).

Remove the skin from the salmon and chop the fish coarsely in a food processor. Add the breadcrumbs, parsley, and egg white and whiz a few more times to combine the mixture. Season to taste. Dampen your hands and roll the mixture into 1-inch (2.5-cm) balls. Chill the salmon balls for 40 minutes.

Place the salmon balls on an oiled baking sheet, drizzle with 2 tsp (10 mL) of the oil, and bake for 15 to 20 minutes or until crisp.

While the salmon balls cook, heat the remaining oil in a saucepan over medium heat. Add the onion and cook, stirring occasionally, until softened, about 10 minutes. Add the curry paste, stir, and let cook for 2 minutes more. Pour in the tomato sauce, add the chili flakes (if using), bring to a boil, and let simmer for 5 minutes. Stir in the lime juice just before serving.

Pour the sauce over the salmon balls and serve.

**PRESENTATION IS EVERYTHING**
Sprinkle a few leaves of cilantro on the surface.

# Oven-Baked Curried Salmon Balls

SERVES 4

1½ lb (750 g) salmon fillet
½ cup (125 mL) fresh
  breadcrumbs
¼ cup (60 mL) chopped parsley
1 egg white
salt and pepper to taste
2 Tbsp (30 mL) vegetable oil
⅔ cup (150 mL) finely chopped
  onion
2 Tbsp (30 mL) purchased curry
  paste
2 cups (500 mL) tomato sauce,
  canned or homemade
dried chili flakes (optional)
2 Tbsp (30 mL) fresh lime juice

# Salmon Rounds with Dill and Lemon Sauce

SERVES 4

4 salmon steaks, about 6 oz
   (170 g) each
salt and pepper to taste
1 Tbsp (15 mL) vegetable oil
1 Tbsp (15 mL) butter
1 Tbsp (15 mL) finely minced
   onion
½ cup (125 mL) whipping cream
1 Tbsp (15 mL) finely chopped
   fresh dill
2 tsp (10 mL) grated lemon rind
lemon wedges for garnish
   (optional)
fresh dill sprigs for garnish
   (optional)

*Salmon steaks are delicious enough in their own right, but when you perform a little knife magic on them, you have a very special dish indeed. You need to shop carefully for the right size of salmon steak. Normally you want the thicker kind. For these salmon rounds, you need the side pieces to be as long as possible so you can roll them into neat little rounds. If you can't, don't panic—they'll still taste good. Buttered noodles and sautéed, thinly sliced zucchini on the side would be my suggestion.*

Cut each salmon steak in half lengthwise. Carefully remove the bones, using tweezers if necessary for the small ones. Coil the long "tail" around the "body" of each steak to create a neat round, and secure with toothpicks. Season to taste.

Heat the oil in a non-stick skillet over medium heat. Add the salmon steaks. Cook for 4 to 5 minutes each side, or until just cooked through. Remove to a heated platter, cover with foil, and keep warm.

Meanwhile, in a small saucepan over medium heat, melt the butter. Add the onion. Turn the heat to medium-low and cook until softened, about 7 minutes. Remove from the heat. Whisk in the cream. Return to the heat, stir in the dill and lemon rind, and cook over medium-low heat until slightly thickened, about 5 minutes. Season to taste with more salt and pepper.

Serve the salmon drizzled with the sauce and accompanied by the lemon wedges (if using) and dill sprigs (ditto).

**PRESENTATION IS EVERYTHING**

Carefully pour the sauce onto a heated oval platter. Arrange the salmon steaks in a neat row down the middle on top of the sauce. Decorate each piece of salmon with a lemon wedge and a dill sprig.

*Round and almost ball-shaped, scallops are so fearfully expensive that I think it's sacrilege to mess about with them. The less you fuss, the more you can appreciate their clean, marine flavor. A satiny soup I ate at Bo, a Hong Kong restaurant that specializes in modern Chinese cuisine, inspired this intriguing combination of tastes. While you're imagining the praise that will come your way, do note that you have to give the orange rind time to infuse, so make the orange oil a few days ahead.*

Heat the creamed corn in a saucepan over low heat. Using the back of a spoon, press the onion through a fine-mesh strainer over the corn so that the onion juice drips in. Stir in the cream, season with salt and pepper, and let cook gently for 5 minutes. Keep warm.

Heat the oil in a non-stick skillet over medium heat. Add the scallops and cook for 2½ to 3 minutes each side until browned, about 5 to 6 minutes in total. They should be barely cooked through in the middle.

Carefully ladle out the creamed corn so it forms a perfect circle on 2 or 4 dinner plates. Position the scallops on top. Drizzle the orange oil around the scallops. Sprinkle with the green onions.

## Orange Oil   MAKES ½ CUP (125 ML)

*Make orange oil a few days before you need it. Don't let leftovers languish in the condiment wasteland at the back of the fridge. Use it in salad dressings (it's delicious with spinach, mandarin oranges, green onions, and almonds) or sprinkle a little over any fish dish. Drizzle it over grilled chicken too.*

½ cup (125 mL) vegetable oil
1 orange, preferably organic, rind removed in long thin strips

Pour the oil into a small glass jar. Add the orange rind and shake well. Leave in the fridge 2 or 3 days for the flavors to permeate the oil.

# Scallops with Orange Oil and Creamed Corn

SERVES 4 AS A STARTER, 2 AS A MAIN COURSE

one 19-oz (540-mL) can
    creamed corn
¼ cup (60 mL) finely chopped
    onion
¼ cup (60 mL) cream
salt and pepper to taste
1 Tbsp (15 mL) vegetable oil
1 lb (500 g) large scallops
3 to 4 tsp (15 to 20 mL) orange
    oil (see below)
1 Tbsp (15 mL) finely chopped
    green onions or chives

**PRESENTATION IS EVERYTHING**
This is a sublimely elegant dish—so use sublimely elegant plates. To be honest, you can't beat those plain white jobbies from Ikea.

# Warm Tuna Boules Niçoise

SERVES 4

two 7-oz (198-g) cans of tuna in
   oil, drained, oil reserved
¼ cup (60 mL) dry breadcrumbs
2 Tbsp (30 mL) coarsely
   chopped black olives
2 Tbsp (30 mL) coarsely
   chopped sun-dried tomatoes
   in oil, drained and patted dry
2 Tbsp (30 mL) finely chopped
   red pepper
2 Tbsp (30 mL) finely chopped
   green onion
1 egg, slightly beaten
salt and pepper to taste
1 Tbsp (15 mL) olive oil

*Most recipes start life with the thought: "What would happen if . . ." In this case, it was having the ingredients for a salade niçoise at hand but, on a chilly winter's night, wanting something cozier. Green beans and steamed potatoes are good accompaniments. Also the Mediterranean peppers on page 53 or ratatouille. And a bottle of red wine.*

Mash the tuna in a bowl until broken up; add the breadcrumbs, olives, sun-dried tomatoes, red pepper, green onion, egg, salt, and pepper. If the mixture looks a little too dry, moisten with the reserved tuna oil. Chill for 30 minutes.

Roll into 1-inch (2.5-cm) balls. Heat the olive oil in a skillet over medium heat. Add the tuna balls and cook until golden on all sides, about 10 minutes.

Serve immediately.

### PRESENTATION IS EVERYTHING

Look to the classic *salade niçoise* for inspiration. Steam tiny new potatoes and hard-cook 2 eggs. Cut the eggs into wedges and set them, along with the potatoes, around the edge of a large warmed plate or platter. Heap the tuna balls in the middle, top with a jaunty cockade of parsley, and have a pot of mayonnaise alongside.

*The proper name for this dish is onigiri and it's a hugely popular traditional Japanese snack food. Onigiri get tucked into lunch boxes too. Among themselves Mama-sans probably call it "making a little salmon go a long way."*

# Japanese Salmon Rice Balls

SERVES 4

2 tsp (10 mL) vegetable oil
½ lb (250 g) salmon fillet
2 tsp (10 mL) soy sauce
salted water
4 cups (1 L) cooked Japanese rice
1 Tbsp (15 mL) sesame seeds, plain or toasted
2 sheets nori, cut into strips

Heat the vegetable oil in a skillet over medium heat. Add the salmon, and cook for 5 to 8 minutes or until just cooked through. Let the salmon cool and flake it with a fork. Drizzle with the soy sauce and mix.

Dip your hands in the salted water and take up approximately ⅓ cup (75 mL) of the cooked rice. Roll into a ball. Make an indentation with your thumb and insert about 1 Tbsp (15 mL) of the salmon. You are making 12 salmon balls so judge accordingly.

Close the rice over the salmon so that it is completely covered. Reshape into a ball and sprinkle lightly with the sesame seeds. Wrap each salmon ball decoratively with the strips of nori, pressing slightly with your fingers so that the seaweed adheres.

**PRESENTATION IS EVERYTHING**
A plain white platter plays up the dark green of the nori. Garnish with the Japanese salad green, mizuna.

**ON THE STREETS OF TOKYO**
The size of golf balls, and grilled in dimpled cast-iron pans, takoyaki are a popular Japanese street snack. Shrimp, octopus, and scallops are the most popular fillings. Crisp outside, moist and light inside, takoyaki are usually garnished with Japanese mayonnaise and bonito flakes.

# Balls Make the World Go Round

# Köenigsberger Klops

SERVES 4

1 lb (500 g) ground beef or pork,
  or a mixture of the two
¾ cup (175 mL) fresh
  breadcrumbs
½ cup (125 mL) finely chopped
  onion
⅓ cup (75 mL) milk
1 egg
1 Tbsp (15 mL) finely chopped
  anchovies
salt and pepper to taste
4 cups (1 L) beef stock
¼ cup (60 mL) butter
¼ cup (60 mL) flour
2 Tbsp (30 mL) lemon juice
2 Tbsp (30 mL) capers in
  vinegar, drained
½ tsp (2 mL) freshly ground
  black pepper

*These German meatballs with their lemony-sharp sauce originated in what used to be the Prussian town of Konigsberg, which is actually now in Russia. End of geography lesson. Either way, they go handsomely with buttery egg noodles or mashed potatoes to sop up the sauce. So does cooked red cabbage, or homemade coleslaw made with cabbage or carrots or both. The anchovies disappear, leaving a depth of flavor.*

Mix together the meat, breadcrumbs, onion, milk, egg, and anchovies in a large bowl. Season to taste and shape the mixture into 1½-inch (4-cm) balls.

Bring the beef stock to a boil in a large saucepan over medium heat. Drop in the meatballs and return the stock to a boil. Lower the heat, and let simmer for 15 minutes or until the meatballs are cooked through. Remove the meatballs to a warmed dish and cover with foil. Reserve 1 cup (250 mL) of the cooking broth for the sauce.

Melt the butter over medium heat in a small saucepan. Whisk in the flour until smooth, and continue cooking for 5 minutes. Remove from the heat and whisk in the reserved cooking broth. Pour this mixture back into the cooking pot and whisk until well mixed.

Add the lemon juice and capers, and bring the mixture to a boil, whisking constantly, until the sauce thickens. Reduce the heat so that the sauce is just simmering. Tip the meatballs back into the sauce, and cook 5 minutes longer or until they are heated through. Add the pepper just before serving.

**PRESENTATION IS EVERYTHING**
Add a fine shower of grated lemon rind over the bowl the minute before you bring it to the table.

Greek food centers on family, friends, and constant feasting with dishes often staying on the table for hours "because you never know who might drop in." Consequently, while excellent hot, many plates are meant to be just as tasty at room temperature. This is only one variation on the popular lamb meatballs served just about everywhere. Pick up hummus, tzatziki, olives, and pita bread at the deli, whip together a classic Greek salad (see sidebar), and supper's ready.

Combine the onion, water, and olive oil in a small saucepan. Bring to the boil and simmer until all the water evaporates. Mix the cooked onion with the breadcrumbs, ground lamb, cumin, oregano, parsley, mint, and vinegar. Season to taste. Form into 1-inch (2.5-cm) balls and chill for 1 hour.

Heat the olive oil in a skillet and add the keftedes. Cook for 15 to 20 minutes, until browned on all sides and cooked through.

## PRESENTATION IS EVERYTHING
Stack on a deep plate, with lemon slices and mint sprigs around the edge.

# Keftedes

SERVES 4

⅓ cup (75 mL) finely chopped onion
3 Tbsp (45 mL) water
2 tsp (10 mL) olive oil
¾ cup (175 mL) fresh, white breadcrumbs
1 lb (500 g) ground lamb
1 tsp (5 mL) ground cumin
1 tsp (5 mL) dried oregano
¼ cup (60 mL) chopped parsley
¼ cup (60 mL) chopped mint
2 tsp (10 mL) red wine vinegar
salt and pepper to taste
1 Tbsp (15 mL) olive oil
mint sprigs for garnish
lemon wedges for garnish

## INSTANT LUNCH
Halve a pita bread and open it up to make a pocket. Add 3 or 4 keftedes, shredded lettuce, sliced tomato and red onion, and a dollop of tzatziki or hummus or both.

## GREEK SALAD
Cut a half cucumber (unpeeled but seeded), a red pepper, half a red onion, and 2 tomatoes into ¾-inch (2-cm) chunks. Combine in a bowl. Sprinkle with 2 tsp (10 mL) oregano, and toss with 2 Tbsp (30 mL) olive oil or to taste. Add ½ cup (125 mL) black olives, ½ cup (125 mL) crumbled feta cheese, and ⅓ cup (75 mL) of chopped parsley. Toss again and serve.

# Frikadeller

SERVES 4

½ lb (250 g) ground pork
½ lb (250 g) ground veal
⅓ cup (75 mL) fresh
    breadcrumbs
⅓ cup (75 mL) sparkling water
1 egg
2 Tbsp (30 mL) finely chopped
    onion
½ tsp (2 mL) ground allspice
salt and pepper to taste
1 Tbsp (15 mL) vegetable oil

As with most northern European spins on the meatball, steamed potatoes and cabbage, or potato salad and coleslaw, round out the meal. Sparkling water lightens these Danish meatballs. I don't know how authentically Danish this is, but cranberry sauce or applesauce on the side also works well. If you can't find ground veal, use all pork.

Combine the meat, breadcrumbs, water, egg, onion, and allspice in a bowl and mix well. Season to taste, and refrigerate the mixture for 30 minutes. Shape the mixture into 1½-inch (4-cm) meatballs.

Heat the vegetable oil in a skillet. Fry the meatballs, turning occasionally, until golden on all sides and cooked through.

**PRESENTATION IS EVERYTHING**
Keep your eyes open at yard sales for Danish pottery from the 1950s.

**BALL PANCAKES**
Obviously fans of spherical foods, Danes often keep an *aebleskiver* pan in their kitchen. Imagine a skillet with a number of round indentations. The pancakes are cooked on top of the stove and traditionally served topped with powdered sugar and raspberry jam.

# Kefta

*Food has scant respect for national boundaries. It simply flows over them and assumes another shape only when the terrain and climate (and hence the availability of local ingredients) change. You find variations on this Lebanese street food all around the Mediterranean. I love cooking them on a chilly night, inhaling the warm spicy aromas of cumin, cinnamon, and allspice that rise up from the pan. They're fairly delicate, so treat them kindly, but don't panic if the occasional chunk breaks off. They'll still taste good.*

1 lb (500 g) ground lamb
¾ cup (175 mL) finely chopped onion
1 Tbsp (15 mL) chopped parsley
1 Tbsp (15 mL) chopped mint
2 tsp (10 mL) ground cumin
1 tsp (5 mL) ground cinnamon
½ tsp (2 mL) ground allspice
salt and pepper to taste
2 Tbsp (30 mL) flour
1 Tbsp (15 mL) olive oil

Combine the ground lamb, onion, and spices in a bowl, mix well, and season to taste. Chill for 1 hour so that the flavors can blend. Shape into 1-inch (2.5-cm) balls. Roll in the flour to coat lightly.

Heat the oil in a skillet over medium heat. Add the kefta and cook, turning occasionally, so they brown on all sides and are cooked through, about 15 minutes.

**PRESENTATION IS EVERYTHING**
I like to serve these with a simple carrot salad, flatbread, and tzatziki made with plain yogurt, chopped cucumber, and loads and loads of torn mint.

# Arancini di Riso

SERVES 4

6 cups (1.5 L) chicken stock
1 pinch of saffron
¼ cup (60 mL) butter
2 Tbsp (30 mL) finely chopped
    onion
1½ cups (375 mL) arborio or
    other risotto rice
⅓ cup (75 mL) white wine or
    dry vermouth (see sidebar)
½ cup (125 mL) freshly grated
    Parmesan cheese
salt and pepper to taste
1 egg, slightly beaten
6 oz (175 g) mozzarella cheese,
    cut in ¼-inch (6-mm) cubes
1½ cups (375 mL) dry
    breadcrumbs
vegetable oil for deep frying

*Arancini is Italian for "little oranges" which tells you something about their size. Originally from Sicily, these rice balls do take time to make but definitely repay the effort in deliciousness. Think of them as classic saffron-scented risotto wrapped around nuggets of—in this case—cheese. Next time you make them, try adding small cubes of ham or salami as well. Mushrooms, shrimp, ham, even a thick ragu can all go inside (but not all at once). Make the arancini ahead of time so they have time to firm up, and alert everyone to stand by so they can devour them the second they're cool enough to eat.*

Heat the stock in a saucepan over medium heat until it is just simmering. Reduce the heat and add the saffron.

Meanwhile, melt the butter in a separate pot over medium heat. Add the onion and stir until it softens, about 5 to 7 minutes. Add the rice and stir well, cooking until the grains become translucent. Pour in the wine and continue cooking until it has almost completely evaporated.

Ladle in approximately 1 cup (250 mL) of the simmering chicken stock. Continue cooking until the rice has almost absorbed all the liquid. Add more stock, let cook as before, and continue until the rice is almost cooked (you may have stock left over). Remove from the heat, stir in the Parmesan, and use the salt and pepper to season.

At this point, you have a classic risotto.

To make the arancini, add the egg to the risotto, mix well, and spread the mixture out on a baking sheet to cool.

Dampen your hands, take up 1 Tbsp (15 mL) of the mixture, and roll it into a ball about the size of a small orange (a little less than 2 inches/5 cm in diameter). Make a dent in the ball with your finger and poke in a few cubes of cheese. Reshape the ball so that the cheese is completely covered. Roll the ball in the breadcrumbs.

Repeat until you have used up all the rice mixture. Chill the arancini on a baking sheet for up to 24 hours.

Pour enough oil into a large, deep-sided skillet so that the arancini will be completely submerged, about 2 inches (5 cm). Heat to 350°F (180°C).

Using a slotted spoon, carefully slide the arancini into the oil. Cook them in batches, turning them as they cook until they are golden brown all over, about 6 minutes.

Drain them on paper towels; let cool for a few minutes before serving.

**WHITE WINE STAND-IN**
If you don't want to open a bottle of Sauvignon Blanc or Pinot Gris just for a recipe, know that dry vermouth (I'm partial to Noilly Prat) works just as well, probably better because of the subtle herby flavors it adds. It lasts, opened, for ages.

# Chiang Mai Pork Balls

SERVES 4

1 lb (500 g) ground pork
⅓ cup (75 mL) finely chopped
   onion
½ cup (125 mL) lime juice
3 Tbsp (45 mL) roasted rice
   powder (see below), or dry
   breadcrumbs
10 tsp (50 mL) fish sauce
   (see page 97)
1 tsp (5 mL) dried chilies
1 tsp (5 mL) finely chopped
   garlic
1 Tbsp (15 mL) vegetable oil
¼ cup (60 mL) thinly sliced
   shallots
2 Tbsp (30 mL) sugar
1 pinch of cayenne pepper
salad greens, steamed rice, or
   cooked rice noodles to serve

**ROASTED RICE POWDER**
My advice would be to look
for it in an Asian grocery store.
You can make it yourself by
heating a heavy skillet (cast
iron is best) over medium heat.
Pour in enough rice just to
cover the bottom. Cook, stirring
occasionally, until the grains of
rice have turned golden brown.
Whiz to a powder in a spice
grinder. Warning: this takes
ages. Breadcrumbs made from
toasted bread are not identical
but they're close.

In Thailand you can eat a superb salad called larb or laap *made with ground chicken or pork. Traditionally, it's served warm with mint, coriander, lettuce, wedges of lime, and scarlet-red chilies. But mixing the meat with all those same gorgeous sharp, sweet, pungent flavors creates terrific meatballs. Warm, or at room temperature, they're very tasty indeed on a salad of shredded lettuce, lots of mint and cilantro, and diced cucumber. Otherwise, serve them hot over rice noodles tossed with the same dressing.*

Combine the ground pork, onion, ¼ cup (60 mL) of the lime juice, the rice powder, 4 tsp (20 mL) of the fish sauce, the chilies, and garlic. Form into 1-inch (2.5-cm) meatballs. There will be liquid left at the bottom of the bowl. Squeeze out any excess moisture from the meatballs.

Heat the vegetable oil in a non-stick skillet over medium heat. Add the pork balls and the sliced shallots. Cook, stirring occasionally, until the meatballs are browned on all sides and cooked through, and the shallots are soft and browned, about 15 minutes. They are quite delicate: use 2 spoons to turn them in the skillet. Remove the meatballs and shallots from the skillet, including any browned bits.

If using the pork balls for a salad, set them aside to cool to room temperature. If eating with rice or noodles, keep warm.

Meanwhile, make the dressing by combining the remaining ¼ cup (60 mL) of the lime juice, sugar, the remaining 2 Tbsp (30 mL) of the fish sauce, and the cayenne in a small bowl.

Toss the dressing with the salad greens, rice, or noodles just before serving, and top with the pork ball and shallot mixture.

*It can get bitterly cold in winter in the high, rugged Pyrenees. Hence a rib-sticking dish like this. Put out a big bowl of egg noodles tossed with a little butter, or steamed potatoes, or that old French standby—a loaf of crusty bread. Can't find sausage meat? Buy your favorite sausages and squeeze them out of their casings.*

Mix together the sausage meat, ground beef, parsley, egg, 1 tsp (5 mL) of the garlic, the spices, salt, and pepper. Flour your hands, form the mixture into 1-inch (2.5-cm) balls, and roll them in the flour.

Heat 1 Tbsp (15 mL) of the olive oil in a skillet over medium heat. Add the meatballs and cook until they are golden brown all over, about 15 minutes. Keep warm.

Meanwhile, make the sauce. In a small saucepan, bring about 2 cups (500 mL) of water to a boil, add the bacon, and blanch for 5 minutes. Drain and dry on a paper towel.

Heat 1 Tbsp (15 mL) more of the olive oil in a large pan. Add the onion and remaining garlic, and cook over medium heat until slightly softened, about 7 to 10 minutes. Add the cooked bacon and tomatoes, bring to a boil, and reduce the heat to low so that the sauce is just simmering.

In a separate skillet over medium heat, heat the remaining 1 Tbsp (15 mL) of olive oil. Add the mushrooms, brown on all sides, and add them to the sauce. Simmer for 15 minutes.

Season to taste with more salt and pepper, add the olives and cooked meatballs, and simmer gently for 20 minutes longer.

### PRESENTATION IS EVERYTHING

A brown pottery casserole. Checked napkins. Bottles of red. A dog under the table. Sheep outside the door.

# Boles de Picolat

SERVES 4

½ lb (250 g) well-seasoned sausage meat
½ lb (250 g) ground beef
¼ cup (60 mL) chopped parsley
1 egg
2 tsp (10 mL) finely chopped garlic
1 pinch of cinnamon
1 pinch of dried chilies
salt and pepper to taste
½ cup (125 mL) flour (approx.)
3 Tbsp (45 mL) olive oil
½ cup (125 mL) chopped bacon
1 cup (250 mL) chopped onion
¾ lb (375 g) ripe tomatoes, peeled, seeded, and coarsely chopped
½ lb (250 g) mushrooms, cut in ½-inch (1-cm) pieces
½ cup (125 mL) pitted green olives

### PEELING AND SEEDING TOMATOES

Run a very sharp knife around the equator of each tomato. Drop it into a pot of boiling water for 30 seconds. Remove and let cool. The skins should slide off as easily as silk underwear. Halve the tomatoes crosswise and scoop out the seeds. Chop the flesh as needed.

# One More Margarita Mexican Meatballs

SERVES 4 TO 6

1 lb (500 g) lean ground beef
½ cup (125 mL) finely chopped
  onion
4 tsp (20 mL) taco seasoning
  mix, or to taste
  (see page 27)
1 tsp (5 mL) finely chopped
  garlic
dried chilies to taste
1 Tbsp (15 mL) vegetable oil
1 cup (250 mL) bottled salsa
bottled hot sauce to taste

*Grinding spices and chopping vegetables for a sauce for Mexican meatballs one day, I realized that someone else had already done the work. Not that I'm usually a fan of prepared spice mixes and bottled sauces, but sometimes—such as when you have a crowd coming, you're tight for time, and you'd rather get into the margs and Dos Equis along with everyone else—it's okay to take a few culinary liberties. Packaged taco seasoning mixes vary enormously in intensity. Do test yours before adding the full quantity specified (or make your own; see page 27).*

In a large bowl, combine the beef, onion, taco seasoning mix, and garlic. Check the seasoning and up the heat with the dried chilies if you like. Form into 1-inch (2.5-cm) balls.

Heat the oil in a non-stick skillet over medium heat. Brown the meatballs on all sides until almost cooked through, about 10 minutes. Lift them out with a slotted spoon and discard any fat. (You can do this up to 24 hours ahead, refrigerating the meatballs until needed.)

Return the meatballs to the skillet, pour in the salsa, and bring to a boil. Reduce the heat to low and simmer uncovered for 10 minutes. Salsa thickness varies. If it looks as though the sauce is becoming too thick, thin with a little water. Add hot sauce to taste.

### PRESENTATION IS EVERYTHING

Serve with any or all of the following: rice, soft tacos, black beans (drained, rinsed, and reheated), avocado, sour cream, shredded Monterey Jack cheese, or chopped olives.

Fair enough. Not being actually ball-shaped, pain bagnat is a bit of a cheat, but this hefty knife-and-fork sandwich was, so they say, created for boules players. Think of it as a portable salade niçoise *that you can carry along in the picnic basket or, on a rainy Sunday, eat in front of the TV while weeping over* Jean de Florette. *Uncork a bottle of Provençal rosé.*

Slice the baguettes lengthwise and scoop out the crumbs (save for other recipes). Peel and halve the garlic clove, and rub it with energy and enthusiasm on the inside of the baguettes. Drizzle with the olive oil.

Layer the lettuce leaves, one-half of the tomato slices, all the cucumber and red onion, and the anchovy fillets on the bottom halves of the baguettes.

Drain the tuna, place it in a bowl, and flake it lightly with a fork. Add the black olives and capers, and mix gently (you don't want to break up the tuna too much). Spoon the tuna mixture onto the baguettes, and top with the remaining tomato slices.

Top with the other halves of the baguettes. Press the sandwich halves together firmly, and wrap them tightly in plastic wrap. Place a large cutting board on top weighed down with canned foods and leave for 2 hours.

At serving time, slice each baguette into 2 pieces.

### PRESENTATION IS EVERYTHING

This is casual food but if you are bringing it out on a serving platter for friends, maybe surround the sandwiches with black olives and parsley sprigs. Plan B is to use a large round loaf of rustic bread instead of baguettes, and cut the result into 4 jaw-challenging wedges.

## Pain Bagnat for Boules Players

SERVES 4

2 baguettes
1 garlic clove
¼ cup (60 mL) olive oil
4 large lettuce leaves
12 slices tomato
12 slices cucumber
½ large red onion, thinly sliced
8 anchovy fillets
two 7-oz (198-g) cans of oil-packed tuna
⅓ cup (75 mL) black olives, stoned and coarsely chopped
⅓ cup (75 mL) capers

### BIRTH OF THE SANDWICH
The original sandwich was designed in the mid-18th century for John Montagu, the Fourth Earl of Sandwich. He didn't like losing good card-playing time to sit down at table, so he requested meat to be brought to him between two slices of bread.

# Mumbai Meatballs

SERVES 4

1 lb (500 g) lean ground beef
¼ cup (60 mL) finely chopped
   onion
2 Tbsp (30 mL) lemon or lime
   juice
1 Tbsp (15 mL) tomato paste
1 Tbsp (15 mL) flour
1 tsp (5 mL) finely chopped
   garlic
½ tsp (2 mL) ground cumin
½ tsp (2 mL) ground coriander
½ tsp (2 mL) chili powder
¼ tsp (1 mL) cayenne pepper
¼ tsp (1 mL) cinnamon
salt and pepper to taste

*This recipe began life as kebabs shaped around wooden skewers. One day I ran out of wooden skewers and discovered it makes good meatballs too. Throw together a raita to go alongside (see sidebar), steam some rice if you've time, or dish it up with purchased roti or naan if you haven't. A salad of shredded lettuce, roughly torn mint, and diced cucumber is nice too. Maybe that jar of mango chutney lurking at the back of the fridge . . . Don't be daunted by what seems to be a lot of ingredients. Once you've pulled down all the right spices (and wondered why so many start with "C"), preparation takes minutes.*

Preheat the broiler.

Mix all the ingredients together in a bowl. Season to taste with the salt and pepper. Dampen your hands and shape the mixture into 1-inch (2.5-cm) balls. Place on the broiler rack on the middle shelf of the oven for 15 minutes, turning every 5 minutes, until browned on the outside and cooked through.

You can also cook these in a skillet, using 1 Tbsp (15 mL) vegetable oil.

### PRESENTATION IS EVERYTHING
On a platter, make a bed of finely shredded lettuce. Arrange the meatballs on top. Garnish with sprigs of cilantro, a trio of fresh hot red peppers, and lemon or lime wedges.

## RAITA
1 cup (250 mL) of yogurt is the base. Optional additions are 1 to 2 Tbsp (15 to 30 mL) of mango chutney and 1 tsp (5 mL) of garam masala. Or add 4 Tbsp (60 mL) of finely chopped cucumber and ½ tsp (2 mL) of finely chopped garlic.

# ...ch Meatballs (Gehaktballen)

SERVES 4

1 lb (500 g) ground beef
½ cup (125 mL) fresh
    breadcrumbs
1 egg
½ tsp (2 mL) grated nutmeg
salt and pepper
¼ cup (60 mL) butter
2 Tbsp (30 mL) tomato ketchup
1 bay leaf
¼ tsp (1 mL) ground cloves

*Dutch food is robust food and this is no exception. In some homes, these meatballs can be so large you only get one per person. They take less time to make but they do take longer to cook. These are smaller but just as good. Serve them with oven-fried chips (see page 65), and mayonnaise or applesauce.*

Mix together the meat, breadcrumbs, egg, and nutmeg. Season to taste and form into 12 meatballs.

Melt the butter in a large skillet over medium-low heat. Add the meatballs and brown on all sides, about 10 minutes. Add the ketchup, bay leaf, and cloves. Cover the skillet, reduce the heat, and let the meatballs simmer for 10 minutes or until cooked through. Check midway to see that they are not drying out, adding a little water if necessary.

**BITTERBALLEN AND BEER**
Stop off in any Amsterdam bar and you'll probably see these *bitterballen* on a snack menu—deep-fried meatballs commonly served with mustard. They're made from a beef or veal ragout left to chill overnight, then scooped and shaped into balls, given a double coating of breadcrumbs, and deep-fried.

One of the key ingredients in this dish is the spicy, fermented, pickled cabbage called kimchee. Asian groceries carry it, but if you can't find it, I heartily advocate making your own. There are lots of recipes online and a splendid one in Madhur Jaffrey's World-of-the-East Vegetarian Cooking. Just be warned, your kitchen will smell of ripening cabbage for a day or so. Rice and stir-fried veggies, with additional kimchee on the side for heat addicts, round this out into a hearty meal.

Preheat the oven to 350°F (180°C).

Combine all the ingredients in a large bowl. Mix well together and shape into 1½-inch (4-cm) meatballs. Line a rimmed baking sheet with foil and stand a cookie rack on it. Place the meatballs on the cookie rack in the center of the oven. Bake for 20 to 25 minutes, flip the balls over, and cook for a further 15 minutes or until done.

**PRESENTATION IS EVERYTHING**
These look and taste very attractive nestled into a bed of Asian greens—which have been stir-fried with fish sauce (see page 97), ginger, and garlic.

# Korean Meatballs

SERVES 4

1¼ lb (625 g) ground beef
¾ cup (175 mL) drained and chopped kimchee
½ cup (125 mL) chopped green onion
1 egg
3 Tbsp (45 mL) flour
1 Tbsp (15 mL) finely chopped garlic
1 Tbsp (15 mL) soy sauce
2½ tsp (12 mL) sesame oil
2 tsp (10 mL) sugar

# Teriyaki Meatballs

SERVES 4

1 lb (500 g) ground beef
¼ cup (60 mL) finely chopped
    green onions
¼ cup (60 mL) teriyaki sauce
1 tsp (5 mL) finely chopped
    ginger
1 tsp (5 mL) finely chopped
    garlic

*Making teriyaki sauce from scratch takes time, but not much time (see below). Or you can use the bottled kind. In either case, this recipe comes together in minutes. Serve with steamed rice, stir-fried greens, and more teriyaki sauce on the side.*

Preheat the oven to 350°F (180°C).

Combine all ingredients in a large bowl. Shape into 1-inch (2.5-cm) balls. Place in a 9- x 11-inch (23- x 28-cm) baking dish on the middle shelf of the oven. Cook for 25 minutes.

Stove-top method: heat 1 Tbsp (15 mL) vegetable oil in a non-stick pan over medium heat. Cook the meatballs until browned and cooked through.

## Homemade Teriyaki Sauce    MAKES ABOUT 1½ CUPS (375 ML)

1¼ cups (310 mL) water
¼ cup (60 mL) soy sauce
3 Tbsp (45 mL) brown sugar
1 Tbsp (15 mL) finely chopped ginger
1 Tbsp (15 mL) finely chopped garlic
2 Tbsp (30 mL) cornstarch

Combine 1 cup (250 mL) of the water, the soy sauce, brown sugar, ginger, and garlic in a pan, stir well, and bring to a boil over medium heat. Reduce the heat and simmer 3 minutes.

Meanwhile whisk together the cornstarch and the remaining ¼ cup (60 mL) of water in a bowl.

Stir the cornstarch mixture into the sauce, and continue whisking until the sauce thickens. If it is too thick for your taste, thin with some water. Keep refrigerated up to 2 weeks.

**PRESENTATION IS EVERYTHING**
A little more chopped green onion, a flask of warmed sake, and you in a kimono.

Dijon mustard, thyme, and green peppercorns give a Gallic accent to the sauce that bathes these simple meatballs. Skip the sauce and you can line them up in a split baguette along with chopped lettuce, sliced tomato, additional mustard, and mayonnaise. The sauced version demands a vinaigrette dressed, crisp green salad and a rustic crusty loaf.

Combine the beef with 2 tsp (10 mL) of the mustard, the thyme, garlic, salt, and pepper. Shape into 1-inch (2.5-cm) balls.

Heat the olive oil and butter in a skillet, and add the meatballs. Brown on all sides, about 15 minutes. Remove the meatballs and keep warm. Pour off the excess fat.

Add the cream to the skillet, along with the green peppercorns and Worcestershire sauce, and heat until slightly thickened. Whisk in the remaining 1 Tbsp (15 mL) of mustard, and pour the sauce over the meatballs. Sprinkle with the chopped chives.

**PRESENTATION IS EVERYTHING**

This isn't fine French cuisine, but the cream sauce does give it a *soupçon* of elegance. Instead of chopped chives, take 2 whole ones and criss-cross them on the top of the boules.

# Boules Provençales

SERVES 4

1 lb (500 g) ground beef
5 tsp (25 mL) coarse Dijon
  mustard
1 tsp (5 mL) finely chopped
  fresh thyme, or ½ tsp (2 mL)
  dried thyme
1 tsp (5 mL) finely chopped
  garlic
salt and pepper to taste
2 tsp (10 mL) olive oil
1 tsp (5 mL) butter
1 cup (250 mL) whipping cream
  or crème fraîche (see
  page 50)
1 Tbsp (15 mL) green
  peppercorns
2 tsp (10 mL) Worcestershire
  sauce
¼ cup (60 mL) chopped chives

# Orange-y Chinese Meatballs

SERVES 4

1 lb (500 g) ground pork
¼ lb (125 g) uncooked shrimp, peeled, deveined, and coarsely chopped
¼ cup (60 mL) finely chopped water chestnuts
¼ cup (60 mL) finely chopped green onion
1 egg, lightly beaten
2 Tbsp (30 mL) cornstarch
2 Tbsp (30 mL) soy sauce
1 piece of dried orange rind soaked in warm water till soft and finely chopped, or 2 tsp (10 mL) grated fresh orange rind
1 tsp (5 mL) sugar
1 tsp (5 mL) finely chopped ginger
2 Tbsp (30 mL) vegetable oil
1 cup (250 mL) chicken stock
½ cup (125 mL) orange juice
4 cups (1 L) shredded bok choy
2 Tbsp (30 mL) water
1 tsp (5 mL) sesame oil

*Dried orange rind is a secret ingredient in daubes in the south of France, and also in some Chinese dishes. In Chinatowns, storekeepers will sell it to you, already dried, from large glass jars. If you can get your hands on it, by all means do. Otherwise, just save the rind from the next orange or tangerine that you eat, and leave it somewhere warm to dry out. If you can't wait to make this dish, use fresh rind.*

Combine the pork, shrimp, water chestnuts, green onion, egg, 1 Tbsp (15 mL) of the cornstarch, 1 Tbsp (15 mL) of the soy sauce, the orange rind, the sugar, and the ginger. Form into 1½-inch (4-cm) meatballs.

Heat the oil over medium heat in a saucepan. Add the meatballs and cook for 10 minutes until they are browned all over. Pour off any excess fat.

Add the chicken stock, orange juice, and remaining 1 Tbsp (15 mL) of soy sauce, and bring to a boil. Reduce the heat, cover the saucepan, and simmer 10 minutes.

Lay the shredded boy choy on top of the meatballs, cover the pot, and cook for 7 minutes longer. Remove the meatballs and bok choy to a heated bowl, leaving the cooking juices behind.

Whisk the remaining 1 Tbsp (15 mL) of cornstarch with the water and stir into the saucepan. Continue to cook until the sauce thickens. Add the sesame oil.

Pour the sauce over the meatballs and bok choy. Serve immediately.

**PRESENTATION IS EVERYTHING**
Add a couple of curlicues of orange rind and a sprinkling of chopped green onion.

The sausages we know and love are either, well, tubular or—as served in fast food outlets—formed into patties. These sausages are neither shape (otherwise they wouldn't be in this book). Traditionally spiced, they are terrific with bacon and fried eggs plus, for the "real English fry-up" experience, Heinz Baked Beanz, mushrooms, a grilled tomato, and cold, leathery toast. You can also serve sausage balls for supper either with mashed spuds or the oven-fried "chips" on page 65. A cold sausage sandwich with tomato ketchup in a baguette for lunch? These little rascals go everywhere.

Soak the breadcrumbs in the milk for 10 minutes. Mix the pork and bacon together in a bowl. Squeeze as much milk as you can from the breadcrumbs, and combine them with the meat mixture.

Add all the remaining ingredients (except for the vegetable oil), season to taste, and mix well.

Heat the vegetable oil in a non-stick skillet over medium heat. Add the sausage balls and cook, stirring occasionally, until they are browned on all sides and cooked through, about 15 minutes.

**PRESENTATION IS EVERYTHING**
Decant the tomato ketchup or HP sauce into attractive bowls. I'm joking. This is everyday fare.

# Cambridge Sausage Balls

SERVES 4

⅓ cup (75 mL) fresh wholegrain breadcrumbs
½ cup (125 mL) milk
1 lb (500 g) ground pork
¼ cup (60 mL) finely chopped bacon
¼ cup (60 mL) finely chopped parsley
2 tsp (10 mL) dried sage
1 tsp (5 mL) dried thyme
1 tsp (5 mL) finely chopped garlic
¼ tsp (1 mL) ground mace
¼ tsp (1 mL) ground allspice
salt and pepper to taste
1 Tbsp (15 mL) vegetable oil

**FAGGOTS AND PEAS**
I debated about including a recipe for this U.K. specialty, then didn't. These days, gourmets don't get too excited about a meatball made, authentically, with piggy leftovers. Traditionally that means liver: simmered, minced, seasoned with sage and onion, then made into balls, wrapped with caul fat, and baked. Anyone who's really keen can use those guidelines. Mushy peas are the classic accompaniment.

## ••• *Vietnamese Meatball Sandwiches*

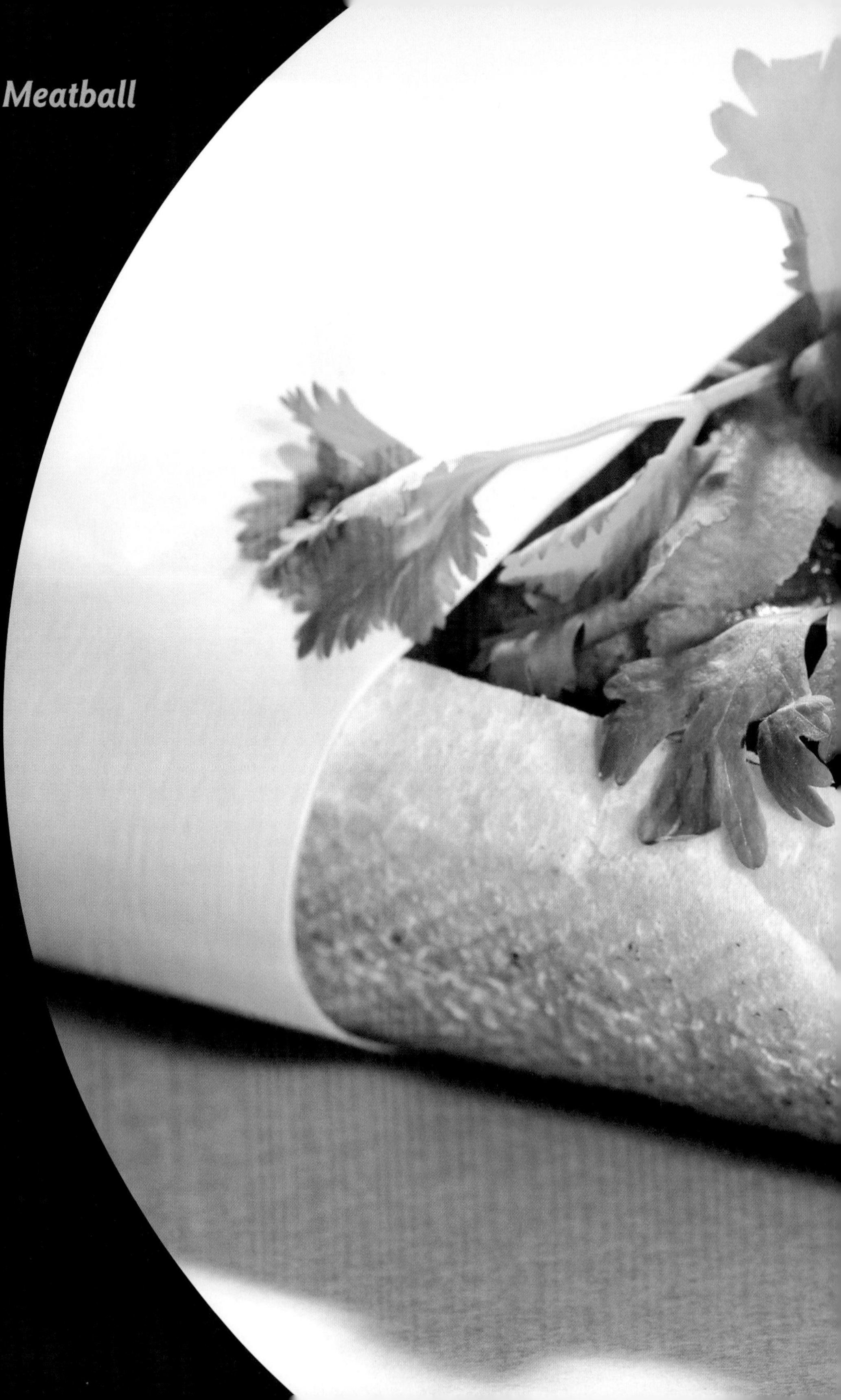

# Vietnamese Meatball Sandwiches

SERVES 4

4 cups (1 L) water
2 Tbsp (30 mL) sugar
1 Tbsp (15 mL) rice vinegar
1½ cups (375 mL) carrot
  ribbons (see sidebar)
1 lb (500 g) ground pork
⅓ cup (75 mL) finely chopped
  onion
1 egg, slightly beaten
2 Tbsp (30 mL) cornstarch
2 Tbsp (30 mL) finely chopped
  cilantro
2 tsp (10 mL) soy sauce
1 tsp (5 mL) freshly ground
  pepper
½ tsp (2 mL) sesame oil
1 Tbsp (15 mL) vegetable oil
¼ cup (60 mL) thinly sliced
  shallot
2 tsp (10 mL) finely chopped
  garlic
2 tsp (10 mL) finely chopped
  jalapeño
1⅓ cups (325 mL) canned
  tomato sauce
2 Tbsp (30 mL) Asian fish sauce
  (see sidebar)
2 French baguettes, or 4 long
  crusty bread rolls
sprigs of cilantro for garnish

When they're made with pork, these are called bánh mì; you'll see them everywhere on the streets of Hanoi or Ho Chi Minh City. Baguettes are a holdover from the French colonial period. Do note that jalapeños vary widely in strength. Before you add the full 2 tsp (10 mL) you might want to try a tiny fragment on the tip of your tongue. If that has you gasping for water, you know what to do.

Make the pickled carrots first. Combine the water, sugar, and vinegar in a large bowl. Add the carrots. Refrigerate for 2 hours or longer. Drain before using.

Preheat the oven to broil.

Combine the pork, onion, egg, cornstarch, cilantro, soy sauce, pepper, and sesame oil in a large bowl. Shape into 1-inch (2.5-cm) meatballs. Place on a broiler pan on the middle shelf and cook for 10 minutes. Turn and cook 10 minutes longer, or until browned and cooked through.

While the meatballs are cooking, make the sauce. Heat the vegetable oil in a medium skillet over medium-low heat. Add the shallot, garlic, and jalapeño, and cook until slightly softened, about 5 minutes. Pour in the tomato sauce, stir well, bring to a boil, reduce the heat, and simmer until the sauce thickens, about 10 minutes. Stir in the fish sauce, set aside, and keep warm.

Slice the baguettes lengthwise without cutting them right through. Set a row of meatballs along the bread. Drizzle some of the tomato sauce over them. Add the pickled carrots and more sprigs of cilantro to taste.

**PRESENTATION IS EVERYTHING**
Wrap the sandwiches tightly in paper napkins with a few inches of bread protruding.

**HOW TO MAKE CARROT RIBBONS**

Strictly speaking, you should julienne the carrots. Depending on your knife skills, you may want to . . . chopchopchopchopchop . . . For the rest of us, it's considerably faster to peel each carrot with a vegetable peeler, then keep peeling (rather like sharpening a fat orange pencil). If you then want to stack the thin ribbons of carrot into a stack and julienne them, go ahead.

**NOTHING FISHY ABOUT FISH SAUCE**

*Nuoc nam* (or *nam pla*) is a thin, brown fish sauce that's a staple of most southeast Asian cuisines. It's made from fermented, salted anchovies but tastes pungent rather than fishy. The most familiar brand is Golden Boy from Thailand, which simply says "fish sauce" on the label.

# Ragoût de Boulettes

SERVES 4

1 Tbsp (15 mL) vegetable oil
   (approx.)
½ cup (125 mL) chopped onion
1 lb (500 g) ground pork
¼ tsp (1 mL) cinnamon
¼ tsp (1 mL) nutmeg
1 pinch of ground cloves
salt and pepper to taste
⅓ cup (75 mL) flour
3 cups (750 mL) strong
   chicken stock (see page 125)
chopped parsley for garnish

*For a time I lived in Montreal enduring brutally cold winters during which comfort food such as this was just what we craved. Like most classic Québécois cuisine, the original recipe for ragoût de boulettes probably came over from France with the first settlers. An unknown land and no central heating. Brrrr . . . The good thick gravy and the hints of nutmeg and cloves warm you to your toes. Serve with potatoes or noodles.*

Heat the vegetable oil in a skillet over medium heat. Add the chopped onion and cook, stirring occasionally, until it turns soft and golden, 7 to 10 minutes. Remove the onion with a slotted spoon, leaving the oil in the skillet.

Combine the ground pork and spices in a large bowl. Add the cooked onions, mix well, and season to taste. Shape into 1½-inch (4-cm) meatballs and roll these boulettes in the flour.

Reheat the skillet over medium heat, adding extra oil if necessary (it should just film the surface). Add the boulettes and cook until browned all over, about 10 minutes. They will continue cooking in the stock.

In a large saucepan, bring the chicken stock to a boil and add the boulettes. Reduce the heat to medium-low, cover, and simmer for 40 minutes.

### PRESENTATION IS EVERYTHING
Garnish with a generous amount of chopped parsley, although I doubt they bothered much with that in early Québécois logging camps.

*The lemon and dill in this version of Swedish meatballs add zest and freshness, which balance the unquestionably rich sauce. Small boiled potatoes and a fruit-based condiment—apple, cranberry, or lingonberry if you are in Sweden or Ikea—round out this family-friendly meal.*

Combine the bread and water, and let soak for 1 minute. Drain and squeeze out excess moisture. Mix together with the beef and pork, onion, egg, dill, lemon rind, and juice. Season to taste with the salt and pepper. Shape into 1-inch (2.5-cm) meatballs.

Melt the butter over medium heat in a skillet. Add the meatballs and brown on all sides. Remove the meatballs, leaving the butter and cooking juices in the skillet.

Meanwhile heat the beef stock in a saucepan. Add the meatballs and let simmer for 10 minutes.

Add the flour to the skillet, whisking well and cooking until it is golden.

Remove the meatballs to a warmed bowl. Stir the broth into the skillet, whisking well until the sauce thickens. Add the sour cream and capers, and cook over low heat for 1 minute.

Pour the sauce over the meatballs.

**PRESENTATION IS EVERYTHING**
Arrange a few sprigs of dill on top of the meatballs.

# Swedish Meatballs with Cream Sauce

SERVES 4

¼ cup (60 mL) fresh
   breadcrumbs
½ cup (125 mL) water
½ lb (250 g) minced beef
½ lb (250 g) minced pork
½ cup (125 mL) finely chopped
   onion
1 egg, slightly beaten
1 tsp (5 mL) chopped fresh dill
1 tsp (5 mL) lemon rind
1 tsp (5 mL) lemon juice
salt and pepper to taste
⅓ cup (75 mL) butter
2 cups (500 mL) beef stock
¼ cup (60 mL) flour
1 cup (250 mL) sour cream
2 Tbsp (30 mL) capers, drained

**SWEDISH MEATBALLS BY THE MILLION**
Shopping at Swedish furniture store Ikea is not for the faint of heart (or tired of foot), which is why company stores worldwide feature a cafeteria where shoppers can pause for a coffee—or a plate of Swedish meatballs. The company says these Scandinavian treats are made by local suppliers using hormone-free beef and pork.

# Vegeta-Balls and Salads

# Mediterranean Falafel

SERVES 4 (2 SANDWICHES PER PERSON)

one 19-oz (540-mL) can of
   chickpeas, drained, rinsed,
   and dried
⅔ cup (150 mL) chopped onion
½ cup (125 mL) chopped
   parsley
2 Tbsp (30 mL) olive oil
2 tsp (10 mL) ground cumin
1 tsp (5 mL) baking powder
1 tsp (5 mL) finely chopped
   garlic
1 tsp (5 mL) freshly squeezed
   lemon juice
1 tsp (5 mL) ground coriander
1 pinch of cayenne pepper
salt and pepper to taste
1 cup (250 mL) dry
   breadcrumbs (approx.)
four 7½-inch (18-cm) pita
   breads, halved and opened
lettuce leaves
sliced tomatoes
sliced red onion
1 cup (250 mL) tzatziki
   (see below), or 1 cup
   (250 mL) plain yogurt
   flavored with tahini to taste

*Generously accessorized, this Mediterranean street food is substantial enough for a week-night supper. But let's be honest here, when stuffed to the limit, these sandwiches make drippy eating. If you want to serve the classic falafel makings deconstructed on a plate and eat them tidily with a knife and fork, go ahead.*

Mash the chickpeas with a fork in a large bowl. Stir in the onion, parsley, 1 Tbsp (15 mL) of the olive oil, cumin, baking powder, garlic, lemon juice, coriander, cayenne, salt, and pepper. Gradually add the breadcrumbs until the mixture loses its stickiness and starts to hold together. Shape into 1-inch (2.5-cm) balls.

Heat the remaining 1 Tbsp (15 mL) of olive oil in a large skillet. Add the falafel balls and cook until browned all over, about 15 minutes. Drain on paper towels.

Place 2 or 3 falafel balls inside each of the halved pita breads, and add lettuce, tomato, onion, and tzatziki or tahini-yogurt to taste.

### PRESENTATION IS EVERYTHING

Distribute the pita breads at one end of a large platter, the tomato and onion slices and lettuce leaves at the other, and the tzatziki in a small bowl in the middle. Heap the falafel around it. Let everyone serve themselves.

## Tzatziki    MAKES ABOUT ½ CUP (100 ML)

1 cup (250 mL) yogurt
½ tsp (2 mL) finely chopped garlic
⅓ cup (75 mL) finely chopped cucumber
¼ cup (60 mL) chopped fresh mint

Just before serving the falafel, mix together.

In our kitchen, canned black beans are a pantry staple. Drained, rinsed, and heated through, they turn fried eggs into a meal (especially with leftover salsa and corn tortillas). Thinned with water or stock and whizzed in the blender, then seasoned with chilis and cumin, they make a fast soup. This dish, with its warming spices, will please vegetarian friends. If they eat cheese, shred some Monterey Jack to serve on the side. Grilled fresh chorizos also go down well, although not of course with herbivores.

# Black Bean Balls with Spicy Sauce

SERVES 4

2 Tbsp (30 mL) vegetable oil
½ cup (125 mL) chopped onion
1 tsp (5 mL) finely chopped garlic
one 19-oz (540-mL) can of black beans, drained (liquid reserved), rinsed, and thoroughly dried
1 Tbsp (15 mL) lime juice
2 tsp (10 mL) chili powder
½ tsp (2 mL) ground cumin
dried chili flakes to taste
salt and pepper to taste
⅓ cup (75 mL) fine cornmeal (approx.)
one 28-oz (796-mL) can of tomatoes, roughly chopped
1 dash of hot sauce, or to taste

Heat 1 Tbsp (15 mL) of the vegetable oil in a skillet over medium-low heat. Add the onion and garlic, and cook, stirring occasionally, for 7 to 10 minutes or until both have softened.

Mash the black beans with a fork in a large bowl. Add the onion and garlic mixture, lime juice, chili powder, and cumin. Season using the chili flakes, salt, and pepper. Gradually mix in enough of the reserved black bean liquid so that the mixture is moist enough to shape into 1-inch (2.5-cm) balls. Roll in the cornmeal to coat.

Heat the remaining vegetable oil in the skillet over low-medium heat. Add the black bean balls and cook, rolling them around so that they are crisp and brown all over and heated through.

Meanwhile, heat the tomatoes in a saucepan over medium heat. Add chili flakes to taste. Simmer for 15 minutes, or until the sauce is reduced and thickened. Adjust heat level with hot sauce to taste. Pour over the cooked balls and serve.

**PRESENTATION IS EVERYTHING**
Bring a basket of hot cornbread, a bowl of lime wedges, and a bucket of cervezas to the table.

# Spinach Salad with Green Apples, Sweet Walnuts, Feta, and Balls-amic Dressing

SERVES 4

⅓ cup (75 mL) olive oil
2 Tbsp (30 mL) balsamic vinegar
salt and pepper to taste
6 cups (1.5 L) spinach, washed and dried
¾ cup (175 mL) cubed, unpeeled Granny Smith apple
½ cup (125 mL) slivered red pepper
⅓ cup (75 mL) crumbled feta cheese
1 cup (250 mL) sweet walnuts (see below)

*The mineral crispness of spinach, the sweet crunch of walnuts, the tang of feta, the bite of tart acid-green Granny Smith apples, and the full-throated sweetness of balsamic dressing. Yum. A salad to cheer you up in the winter months. Make the sweet walnuts ahead of time.*

Whisk the oil, vinegar, and seasonings together in a small bowl. Set this dressing aside.

Combine the spinach, apple, and red pepper in a large serving bowl. Toss with the prepared dressing. Sprinkle the sweet walnuts and feta cheese on top.

**PRESENTATION IS EVERYTHING**

Because this is such a showstopper with its shades of green, scarlet, caramel brown, and cream, display it in all its glory on a big plate (not in a bowl).

## Sweet Walnuts   MAKES 1 CUP (250 ML)

1 cup (250 mL) walnut halves
⅓ cup (75 mL) sugar

Place the walnuts and sugar in a non-stick skillet over medium heat. Stir constantly until the sugar begins to melt around the walnuts. Immediately take the skillet off the heat and tip the walnuts onto a piece of foil. Spread them out into a single layer. Let cool completely, break apart, and store in a lidded jar until needed.

**A WORD ON FETA**
Feta cheese can be crumbly or almost as moist as goat cheese. Either kind works.

# Brussels Sprouts with Bacon

SERVES 4 AS A SIDE DISH

1 lb (500 g) frozen Brussels
   sprouts
⅓ cup (75 mL) coarsely
   chopped bacon
1 tsp (5 mL) finely chopped
   garlic
salt and pepper to taste
½ cup (125 mL) chicken stock

*Peeling Brussels sprouts is one of the most fiddly kitchen tasks there is. As if removing all the outer foliage wasn't enough, you're then meant to cut a little X in the base of each one so they'll cook evenly. On the other hand, you tip frozen sprouts into boiling water. The more you eat them (and being a cruciferous vegetable, they're very good for you) the more you'll like them—and you're less likely to serve them if they're a pain to prepare. I say, go with frozen.*

Drop the sprouts into a pan of boiling water and cook according to package directions (usually for 4 to 5 minutes). Drain, set aside, and keep warm.

While the sprouts cook, heat a skillet over medium heat and fry the bacon until it is just starting to crisp. Add the garlic and cook for 2 minutes longer (be careful not to burn the garlic). Tip the pan so that the bacon fat runs to one side, and remove it either with a turkey baster or by blotting it up with a paper towel.

Return the Brussels sprouts to the pan and sauté them until they just start to brown. Season to taste with the salt and pepper.

Pour in the chicken stock and bring to a boil. Continue to simmer until the stock is almost completely reduced—so there is just enough left to coat the Brussels sprouts.

### PRESENTATION IS EVERYTHING
This dish already has oil and bacon fat in it, so you might as well go whole hog and add a generous dollop of butter just before you bring the sprouts to the table.

# Pois Vichyssoise

*"Vichyspoise" was one name I thought of for this fresh and tasty summer soup, but it's hard to say after a couple of glasses of chilled white wine—which is what you'd probably drink with the grilled chicken or salmon that would follow this dish so beautifully. We should all make cold soups more often.*

1½ cups (375 mL) frozen peas, thawed
1 cup (250 mL) chicken or vegetable stock
1 cup (250 mL) half-and-half (10%) cream
½ cup (125 mL) finely chopped celery
¼ cup (60 mL) finely shredded lettuce
1 Tbsp (15 mL) chopped fresh mint
salt and pepper to taste
4 mint leaves for garnish

Combine all the ingredients (except the mint leaves) in a blender or food processor, and buzz until smooth. Or tip all the ingredients into a bowl and use a hand-held blender. Chill until serving time. Ladle out the vichyssoise into 4 soup bowls and garnish each with a mint leaf.

### PRESENTATION IS EVERYTHING

If you have a large footed glass bowl lurking at the back of the cupboard, your soup will look sensational in it. In which case, use 3 mint leaves, not 4, or every designer in the city will knock you off their Christmas card list.

*Even quite high-end chefs will confess to a reliance on frozen peas. Because, unless you can get your hands on just-picked pods, and shell and cook them immediately, fresh ones quickly turn starchy. This is one of those recipes where the results are far more than the sum of the parts, as everyday ingredients work magic. Try these alongside a crisp roast chicken and pan-fried potatoes.*

## Peas French Style

SERVES 4 AS A SIDE DISH

1 lb (500 g) frozen peas
1 cup (250 mL) shredded
    lettuce leaves
⅔ cup (150 mL) water
¼ cup (60 mL) thinly sliced
    green onions
½ tsp (2 mL) sugar
½ tsp (2 mL) lemon juice
2 Tbsp (30 mL) butter

Place all the ingredients except the butter in a medium-sized pan. Bring to the boil over medium-high heat. Reduce the heat, cover, and simmer for 8 minutes. Drain.

Transfer the peas to a warmed serving bowl. Dot with the butter and serve.

**PRESENTATION IS EVERYTHING**
Adorn with a curl of lemon rind.

# Chickpeas Chennai Style

SERVES 4 AS A SIDE DISH, 2 AS A MAIN COURSE

2 Tbsp (30 mL) vegetable oil
1 cup (250 mL) finely chopped
   onion
1 Tbsp (15 mL) finely chopped
   ginger
2 tsp (10 mL) finely chopped
   garlic
1 tsp (5 mL) ground cumin
1 tsp (5 mL) ground coriander
½ tsp (2 mL) dried chili peppers
¼ tsp (1 mL) cayenne pepper, or
   to taste
one 19-oz (540-mL) can
   chickpeas, drained, liquid
   reserved
¼ cup (60 mL) cilantro,
   chopped for garnish

*A main course if you're vegetarian. Something to go on the same plate as grilled pork chops or chicken thighs, if you're not. In any case, you'll need a little moisture. Mango chutney works well or that all-purpose Thai sweet chili sauce. This is the kind of useful dish you can serve hot, at room temperature, cold, or the following day. Keep that in mind next time you're invited to a potluck supper.*

Heat the oil in a large skillet over medium heat. Turn the heat to low. Add the onion, ginger, garlic, and spices. Cook, stirring often, for 6 to 7 minutes or until the onion softens. Add the chickpeas. Continue cooking until the mixture is heated through, adding a little chickpea liquid if the mixture starts to look dry. Tip into a serving dish and strew with the cilantro.

*Garlic-y, nutty, and smooth, hummus is an insanely convenient dip to keep in the fridge. Bring it out with crackers or pita, and it's a snack while you're catching up on the events of the day (either theirs or the ones on the news). Add salad and it's lunch. Here, hummus's flavor is ratcheted up with cayenne and hot sauce, and colored a warning scarlet with puréed red peppers. Note that if you let canned black beans stand in for the chickpeas and skip the tahini, you're on your way to a dip tailor-made for taco chips.*

Throw everything into the food processor and blend until smooth. Thin with chickpea liquid until of ideal scooping consistency.

**PRESENTATION IS EVERYTHING**

Spoon the hummus into a small bowl. Place it at plate center, and circle with pita triangles that have been baked for 15 minutes at 350°F (180°C) on the center shelf of the oven.

# Hellishly Hot Hummus

### MAKES ABOUT 1¾ CUPS (425 ML)

one 19-oz (540-mL) can chickpeas drained, liquid reserved
2 red peppers, roasted, peeled, and seeded (see sidebar)
3 Tbsp (45 mL) lime juice
1 Tbsp (15 mL) tahini
1 tsp (5 mL) finely chopped garlic
½ tsp (2 mL) ground cumin
½ tsp (2 mL) hot sauce, or to taste
¼ tsp (1 mL) cayenne pepper, or to taste
salt to taste

**NEW PANTRY STAPLE: ROASTED RED PEPPERS**
Glossy as scarlet patent shoes, roasted red peppers are a cinch to make. Broil them on a rimmed baking sheet on the top shelf of the oven, turning until they are blackened on all sides. Transfer them to a heatproof bowl and cover with plastic wrap. Once they're cool, skin each pepper, open it up, and scrape out the seeds and interior gunk (do this over a bowl so you catch all the juices). Pour the juices over the skinned red peppers and refrigerate. Make lots—they will keep for a week in the fridge, ready to go into pasta sauces or dips. I like them in sandwiches too, mainly because their fleshiness lets me cut back on those boosters of personal fleshiness: butter and mayo.

# Beet, Feta, and Walnut Salad

SERVES 4 AS A MAIN COURSE, 6 TO 8 AS A STARTER

¼ cup (60 mL) olive oil, or half-
and-half olive and walnut oils
4 tsp (20 mL) red wine vinegar
salt and pepper to taste
6 cups (1.5 L) arugula or
watercress
1½ cups (375 mL) cooked, diced
beets (see sidebar)
⅔ cup (150 mL) walnut pieces,
toasted
½ cup (125 mL) creamy feta
cheese, diced

*A delectable salad to make in the summer when farmers' markets are bursting with fresh local produce. Use unusual beets, such as yellow or candy-striped varieties, if you can find them. A word of caution: don't make this dish too far in advance or the beets' crimson juices will bleed into the feta—and it's the contrast you're after.*

Whisk together the oil and vinegar, and season to taste. Toss the arugula with half the salad dressing, and distribute on individual plates or a large platter. Just before serving, top with the beets, walnuts, and feta. Drizzle with the remaining dressing.

### PRESENTATION IS EVERYTHING

The combination of the dark green, gold-brown, crimson, and white is attractive enough in its own right. If you can find some tiny red-veined beet greens to include too . . .

### COOKING BEETS

Beet juice stains everything. Roasting is the least messy way to deal with them. Scrub each beet clean, then loosely wrap each one in foil and bake at 400°F (200°C) or until cooked through (figure 45 minutes and up). Obviously the larger the beet, the longer it takes. Let cool, unwrap, and peel. You'll still end up with Lady Macbeth hands, but less so than if you had peeled raw beets. Roasting also keeps all that vibrant color inside the beet instead of letting it leach into the water.

### BEET GREENS: THE "FREE" VEGETABLE

If you're lucky, your beets will come with their greens still attached, giving you two vegetables for the price of one. Cut off the greens, rinse and dry them, and roughly chop any overly big leaves. Sauté them in olive oil until wilted. Either toss the cooked greens with salad dressing and eat at room temperature, or serve them hot as a side dish, drizzled with a little olive oil.

# Cheery Cherry Tomatoes

SERVES 4

*Ta-da. The Only Vegetable Trick You Need to Know is that stir-fried cherry tomatoes go with everything. Chicken, fish, beef, lamb, tofu—you tell me one chunk of protein they won't be happy with. And quick? Just toss them around over the heat for a few minutes and they're ready. Use olive oil if you want to eat them at room temperature, butter if you're bringing them straight to the table.*

1 Tbsp (15 mL) olive oil or butter
2 cups (500 mL) cherry tomatoes
2 tsp (10 mL) chopped fresh herbs
1 Tbsp (15 mL) chopped parsley

Heat the olive oil in a skillet over medium heat. Add the tomatoes and herbs. Cook, stirring frequently, until the tomatoes soften and are a little browned in places. It's all right if some of them burst. Serve topped with the chopped parsley.

**PRESENTATION IS EVERYTHING**

If I was serving these as more of a side salad, I might expand the chopped parsley into gremolata dizzy with lemon rind and garlic (for recipe, see page 124). Or I might add small sprigs of fresh thyme or rosemary. Hot or cold, this dish is dazzling made with equal numbers of red and yellow cherry tomatoes, with torn basil strewn over it at the last moment.

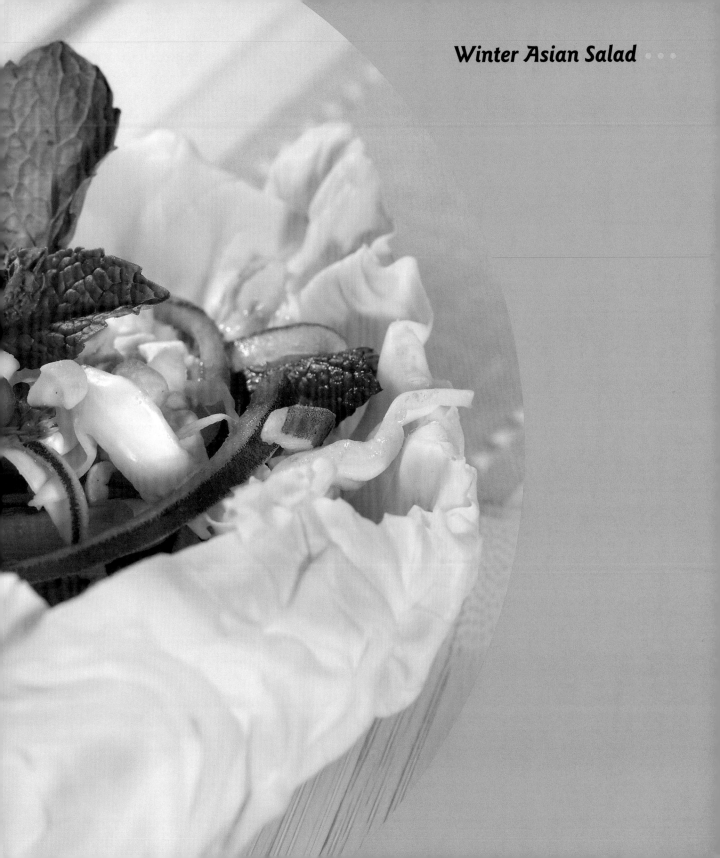

# Winter Asian Salad

SERVES 4

2 Tbsp (30 mL) lime juice

2 Tbsp (30 mL) sweet chili sauce

1 Tbsp (15 mL) fish sauce (see page 97)

1 tsp (5 mL) sugar

4 cups (1 L) shredded green cabbage

1 cup (250 mL) carrot ribbons (see page 97)

½ cup (125 mL) cilantro leaves

½ cup (125 mL) torn fresh mint leaves

⅓ cup (75 mL) thinly sliced red onion

3 Tbsp (45 mL) coarsely chopped peanuts

*I'm all for using local produce as much as I can, which means that, while the occasional long-distance-traveled romaine does show up on our table in the colder months, I'd rather look to variations on cabbage salad. Slaws, sometimes, but more often fresh-tasting Asian versions like this. Obvious partners are Vietnamese (page 96), or Chiang Mai (page 82) meatballs. Adding grilled chicken or shrimp (which you can cook while you're making the salad) are other tricks that transform it into a fast one-bowl supper.*

Mix the lime juice, chili sauce, fish sauce, and sugar in a small saucepan, and place over medium heat until the sugar dissolves. Set this dressing aside and keep warm.

Mix together the cabbage, carrot ribbons, cilantro, mint, and onion in a large bowl. Toss with the dressing and top with the chopped peanuts.

### PRESENTATION IS EVERYTHING

A blue-and-white bowl or platter from Chinatown looks good, especially if you stand it on a bamboo place mat.

### FREE MINT PLANTS

If you bought your mint at a market or store, set aside a couple of sprigs before you start chopping. Place them in a glass of water, and chances are high they'll soon put out little roots. Install your new plants in a pot of soil, but don't let them loose in the garden—mint tends to run riot.

*It's high in fiber, low in calories. Good for you, in other words. Theoretically kohlrabi should be a mainstay of winter cooking, so why do we pass it by? Maybe because those protuberances make it look a little . . . alien? Sometimes it comes with leaves attached: even weirder. It's a shame because kohlrabi's gentle peppery flavor—turnip meets cabbage—can grow on you. Give it a try, maybe sliced thinly in a stir fry or shredded here in this variation on the familiar slaw (which, by the way, is excellent with holiday ham leftovers).*

3 cups (750 mL) peeled and shredded kohlrabi
1½ cups (375 mL) peeled and shredded carrot
2 Tbsp (30 mL) finely chopped onion
⅓ cup (75 mL) sour cream
⅓ cup (75 mL) mayonnaise
4 tsp (20 mL) lemon juice
1 Tbsp (15 mL) Dijon mustard
⅓ cup (75 mL) chopped fresh dill
⅓ cup (75 mL) chopped parsley
ground white pepper to taste

Combine the kohlrabi, carrot, and onion in a large bowl.

Whisk together the sour cream, mayonnaise, lemon juice, and mustard. Toss with the kohlrabi mixture. Add the chopped dill and parsley and toss again. Season with white pepper to taste.

## CELERIAC BISTRO-STYLE
Another big, lumpen ball of a vegetable, the knobbly celeriac (or celery root) also languishes at the back of the produce counter, cheap and unloved, until some savvy and sophisticated type who has been to France picks it up. Ugly though it may look, with its celery-like flavor celeriac makes wonderful soups and purées, can be grated in salads, and is the delicious base for the classic French bistro hors d'oeuvre called *celeri remoulade*. Cut the celeriac into matchsticks, and toss with the same sour cream, mayonnaise, mustard, and lemon juice dressing used in the kohlrabi recipe.

**COPING WITH KOHLRABI**
If you're not intending to use your kohlrabi right away, cut off its leaves or they'll sap its energy. Peel kohlrabi just before you cook it.

# Rutabaga a.k.a. Neeps (and Tatties)

SERVES 4 AS A SIDE DISH

2 cups (500 mL) peeled, cubed
    rutabaga
2 cups (500 mL) peeled, cubed
    potatoes
3 Tbsp (45 mL) butter, softened
¾ cup (175 mL) milk, warmed
    (approx.)
salt and pepper to taste

*Was there ever an uglier name for a vegetable? It sounds rough, cloddish, doltish—no wonder nobody gets excited about the rutabaga. In my native England, we call it a swede. Allegedly it was brought over from Sweden to Scotland (where it became known as a neep), then plodded its stolid way through the rest of the U.K. before being distributed around the colonies. Neeps and tatties are a traditional accompaniment to haggis. Rutabaga goes handsomely with grilled sausages, or Ragoût de Boulettes (page 98).*

Bring 2 pots of water to the boil. Add the rutabaga cubes to one and the potatoes to the other. Cook until both can be pierced with a fork, about 15 minutes. Mix the 2 vegetables together, mash together with the butter, and gradually add the milk (you may not need all of it) until you have a smooth purée. Season to taste.

**PRESENTATION IS EVERYTHING**
Place in a warmed dish, and make horizontal rows of fork marks across the top so it looks like a miniature ploughed field.

**NASTY LITTLE FACTOID**
If you read the fine print on cheap Christmas cakes and puddings, you'll often see rutabaga listed as an ingredient, standing in for more expensive candied fruit.

# Glazed Turnips

*If a haute couture designer was asked to create a vegetable, the result might be the nubile turnip with its elegant white body, purple top, and green topknot. Seek turnips out at farmers' markets. (P.S. As with beets, you can eat the leaves too.) Ideally, they shouldn't be much bigger than golf balls for this recipe. Larger turnips are best either mashed with butter and cream, or chunked and roasted.*

1 lb (500 g) small turnips, washed, trimmed, and quartered
1 Tbsp (15 mL) butter
1 Tbsp (15 mL) olive oil
2 tsp (10 mL) sugar

Drop the turnips into boiling water for 7 minutes or until almost cooked (stick a fork in them to see).

Melt the butter and oil in a skillet. Add the turnips and sprinkle with the sugar. Cook, tossing occasionally, until the turnips are glazed and cooked through.

**PRESENTATION IS EVERYTHING**
Roast duck and turnips are made for each other.

# Fancy Balls of the Savory Kind

# Boules Bourguignon

SERVES 4

¾ cup (175 mL) breadcrumbs
1 cup (250 mL) red wine
1 lb (500 g) ground beef
⅓ cup (75 mL) chopped onion
1 tsp (5 mL) finely chopped
  garlic
salt and pepper to taste
⅓ cup (75 mL) flour (approx.)
⅓ cup (75 mL) chopped bacon
4 cups (1 L) beef stock
½ tsp (2 mL) dried thyme
1 bay leaf
1 sprig of parsley
¾ cup (175 mL) quartered
  mushrooms
¾ cup (175 mL) small onions

*The advantage here is that you don't need to re-member to marinate the meat the night before. Also it's cheaper than the conventional version. Other than ground instead of stewing beef, ingredients are faithful to grandmaman's original recipe. Cooking time is faster; the meat and sauce are cooked separately, then given an oppor-tunity to share flavors. Adding wine-soaked breadcrumbs gives the meatballs an authentic French accent.*

Preheat the oven to 325°F (160°C).

Sprinkle the breadcrumbs with ½ cup (125 mL) of the wine and let soak for 5 minutes. Squeeze the breadcrumbs (saving the wine), and mix them with the ground beef, onion, garlic, salt, and pepper in a large bowl. Shape into 1½-inch (4-cm) balls. Roll in the flour.

Cook the bacon bits in a large ovenproof pot until crisp. Remove the bacon bits, leaving the bacon fat in the pot, and set aside. Brown the meatballs in the bacon fat.

Heat the stock and remaining wine (including the wine from the bread-crumbs) in a separate pot, just until simmering.

Pour the wine and stock mixture over the browned meatballs, add the herbs, cover, and place in the oven on the middle shelf for 30 minutes.

Add the mushrooms and small onions, and cook 20 minutes lon-ger. Adjust seasoning to taste with more salt and pepper and serve immediately.

**PRESENTATION IS EVERYTHING**
Lay a rustic sprig or two of thyme on the surface, and bring the casserole bubbling to the table.

*Another classic of the French farmhouse table, coq au vin was originally designed to use up tough old chickens that had ended their egg-laying days. As with the take on boeuf bourguignon, this recipe captures the spirit of the original but with far less fuss. Serve it with steamed new potatoes, buttered noodles, or rice.*

Brown the bacon in a skillet over medium heat and set aside. Discard the bacon fat but keep the skillet handy.

Toss the chicken pieces with the flour, salt, and pepper. Heat 1 Tbsp (15 mL) of the olive oil in the same skillet and brown the chicken pieces.

Add up to 1 Tbsp (15 mL) of the remaining olive oil if necessary. Add the carrots, onion, shallots, and garlic and sauté, stirring often, for 5 minutes or until slightly softened.

Return the bacon and chicken to the skillet; stir in the chicken stock, wine, and tomato paste. Add the herbs and season to taste. Bring to a boil, reduce the heat, cover the skillet, and let simmer very gently for 20 minutes. Add the mushrooms and continue to cook for a further 15 minutes.

Garnish with the chopped parsley.

# Boules de Coq au Vin

SERVES 4

½ cup (125 mL) chopped bacon
2 lbs (1 kg) skinless boneless chicken thighs, cut into 1½-inch (4-cm) chunks
2 Tbsp (30 mL) flour
salt and pepper to taste
2 Tbsp (30 mL) olive oil (approx.)
¾ cup (175 mL) thickly sliced carrots
⅔ cup (150 mL) coarsely chopped onion
¼ cup (60 mL) coarsely chopped shallots
1 tsp (5 mL) finely chopped garlic
1½ cups (375 mL) strong chicken stock (see page 125)
1 cup (250 mL) red wine
2 Tbsp (30 mL) tomato paste
1 sprig of fresh thyme, or ½ tsp (2 mL) dried thyme
1 sprig of fresh parsley
1 bay leaf
salt and pepper to taste
¾ cup (175 mL) quartered mushrooms
2 Tbsp (30 mL) chopped parsley

# Meatballs Osso Bucco Style

*Why does everything sound so much better in Italian? Osso bucco basically means "bone with a hole." Traditionally it's made with lengths of veal shank, but as the dish shows up increasingly on trendy dinner tables, the price of this former budget meat has rocketed. While the meat is part of authentic osso bucco, so is the marrow. Using chicken stock so strong that it sets into jelly when it's cold helps recreate the meaty feel. Risotto (see next page) is the traditional accompaniment.*

Preheat the oven to 350°F (180°C).

Mix the meat with the breadcrumbs and the egg in a bowl, and season to taste. Shape into 2-inch (5-cm) balls and roll in the flour.

Heat 1 Tbsp (15 mL) of the olive oil in a large, heavy, ovenproof skillet, and sauté the meatballs until browned all over. Remove and keep warm.

Heat the remaining olive oil and the butter over medium heat, and sauté the onion for 5 minutes. Add the celery, carrot, and garlic and sauté for 2 to 3 minutes longer. Pour in the tomatoes, chicken stock, wine, and sugar and stir well. Season to taste with more salt and pepper.

Return the meatballs to the skillet, cover, and place in the oven for 40 minutes. Uncover and continue cooking for 20 minutes so that the sauce reduces slightly. If not quite thick enough, lift out the meatballs with a slotted spoon and keep warm on a dish, tented with cooking foil. Bring the sauce to a boil and simmer until thickened, then pour it over the meatballs.

Just before serving, mix the lemon rind, garlic, and parsley together to make the gremolata, and sprinkle over the meatballs.

**PRESENTATION IS EVERYTHING**

With its own reds and browns, and the green, white, and citric yellow of the gremolata, this is a rustic looking dish. Bring it to the table in the cast iron skillet you cooked it in.

**RISOTTO: THE DISH THAT MAKES ITS OWN SAUCE**

Osso bucco is traditionally served with creamy risotto. Use the recipe on page 80.

**CHICKEN STOCK MADE SIMPLE**

Strong chicken stock is made by simmering regular-strength chicken stock in an uncovered pot until it reduces by one-half or more. Chicken stock is made by covering chicken bones—raw (and rinsed) or cooked—with water. Bring to a slow simmer and let cook for 1 hour, spooning off any nasty gray scum that appears. Strain the chicken stock and refrigerate so you can lift off any hardened fat the next day. You can also boil the chicken stock to concentrate its flavor (it should be thick enough to set into a jelly) and freeze in an ice cube tray. To use each concentrated cube, add 1 cup (250 mL) of water.

# Meatballs Stroganoff

SERVES 4

1 lb (500 g) ground beef
salt and pepper to taste
1 Tbsp (15 mL) vegetable oil
1 Tbsp (15 mL) butter
½ cup (125 mL) finely chopped
  onion
1 Tbsp (15 mL) flour
⅔ cup (150 mL) beef or chicken
  stock
1 cup (250 mL) thinly sliced
  mushrooms
1 dash of Worcestershire sauce
⅓ cup (75 mL) sour cream or
  crème fraîche (see page 50)
2 Tbsp (30 mL) chopped
  parsley

*Made with beef fillet as it was originally, this is a costly dinner. Using ground beef puts it into budget country. This luxe dish was first invented in the 1890s in St. Petersburg by the chef in the employ of a certain Count Stroganoff. When the dish won a cooking contest, the chef did the wise thing and named it after his boss. Legend has it that the count had bad teeth, which made it impossible for him to chew regular steak.*

Season the beef to taste, and roll into 1-inch (2.5-cm) balls. Heat the vegetable oil in a skillet over medium heat and cook, stirring occasionally, until the meatballs are browned on all sides and cooked through, about 15 minutes. Remove the meatballs to a warmed serving dish and keep warm.

Wipe out the skillet, melt the butter over medium-low heat, add the onion, and cook until softened, about 5 minutes. Reduce the heat to low and stir in the flour with a wooden spoon until it is well blended. Let cook gently for about 3 minutes.

Pour in the stock and bring to a boil so that it thickens, reduce the heat, and add the mushrooms and Worcestershire sauce. Let simmer 5 to 7 minutes longer or until the mushrooms are just cooked through.

Remove the skillet from the heat and stir in the sour cream. Add the meatballs and heat gently so that the sauce can warm through. Season to taste with more salt and pepper, sprinkle with the parsley, and serve.

**PRESENTATION IS EVERYTHING**
Noodles on the side look very handsome if you toss them with butter and 1 tsp (5 mL) of black poppy seeds just before serving.

A menu chalked on a blackboard, a pichet of vin rouge, a plain white plate loaded with steak frites, and a creamy sauce. This is the kind of meal you see in little cafés all over France. It's not the kind of meal you try to duplicate at home. Keeping an eye on a number of steaks' degree of doneness while monitoring a deep fryer is too much like hard work. Here, a periodic shake of the meatball pan, a leisurely turning of the frites, and a little last minute work with whisk and whipping cream is all it takes.

Preheat the oven to 350°F (180°C).

Combine the ground beef and egg in a bowl, and season to taste with the salt. Shape into 1-inch (2.5-cm) meatballs and sprinkle with the coarsely ground black pepper. Set aside.

Cut each potato lengthwise into 8 wedges. Place the vegetable oil, pepper, and more salt to taste in a plastic bag. Add the potato wedges and scrumple them around until they are evenly coated with oil and seasonings. Tumble onto a rimmed baking sheet, and place on the middle shelf of the oven. Cook for 20 minutes. Turn, and cook for 20 minutes longer.

While the frites finish cooking, heat the olive oil in a skillet over medium heat and add the prepared meatballs. Cook, turning occasionally, until they are browned all over and cooked through, about 15 minutes. Remove to a warmed dish and tent with foil.

Get rid of any excess fat in the skillet (but leave any delicious browned bits), melt the butter, add the shallots, and cook until softened, about 5 to 7 minutes. Add the stock, bring to a boil, and let cook until reduced by one-half. Add the brandy (if using) and the cream, reduce the heat to low, and cook for 1 minute longer so that the sauce thickens slightly.

**PRESENTATION IS EVERYTHING**
Candles, red wine—you know the drill.

# Bistro "Steak" with Oven Frites

SERVES 4

1 lb (500 g) lean ground beef
1 egg
salt to taste
1 Tbsp (15 mL) cracked black peppercorns
3 large baking potatoes, unpeeled
¼ cup (60 mL) vegetable oil
pepper to taste
1 Tbsp (15 mL) olive oil
2 Tbsp (30 mL) butter
¼ cup (60 mL) finely chopped shallots or onion
⅔ cup (150 mL) beef stock
1 Tbsp (15 mL) brandy (optional)
½ cup (125 mL) whipping cream

# Pork Balls with Prune-Cream Sauce

SERVES 4

1 cup (250 mL) red wine
1 cup (250 mL) dried pitted
  prunes
1 lb (500 g) ground pork
⅓ cup (75 mL) fresh
  breadcrumbs
½ tsp (2 mL) dried thyme
salt and pepper to taste
⅓ cup (75 mL) flour (approx.)
1 Tbsp (15 mL) olive oil
⅔ cup (150 mL) chopped onion
1 tsp (5 mL) finely chopped
  garlic
1 cup (250 mL) chicken stock
½ cup (125 mL) whipping cream
  or crème fraîche
  (see page 50)
1 Tbsp (15 mL) Dijon mustard
2 Tbsp (30 mL) chopped
  parsley

Pork gets along remarkably well with fruit: oranges, apples, plums or, as here, prunes. This particular marriage is a popular one in rural France, especially around the southern town of Agen (famed for its plump, juicy prunes). Most recipes for this dish call for expensive pork fillet. Making it with ground pork delivers all the flavor at a fraction of the cost. Serve with rice, egg noodles, or bread. Soak the prunes overnight before making this dish.

Warm the red wine in a pan, add the prunes, and let them soak for 1 to 2 hours or overnight.

Mix together the ground pork, breadcrumbs, thyme, salt, and pepper. Shape into 1-inch (2.5-cm) meatballs and roll in the flour.

Heat the olive oil in a skillet. Add the onion and garlic, and cook until softened, about 5 minutes. Add the meatballs and brown on all sides, 10 to 15 minutes. Remove any excess fat with a turkey baster.

Add the prunes in wine and the chicken stock, bring to a boil, and simmer for 10 minutes or until the meatballs are cooked through. Remove the meatballs to a warmed platter.

Whisk the cream and Dijon mustard into the sauce. Bring to a boil and simmer until slightly thickened. Pour over the meatballs.

Sprinkle with the chopped parsley.

VOILÀ! DESSERT
Prunes are like people. If you soak them in booze—red wine, brandy, port—they grow soft and fat. Store them in a lidded jar, then spoon over ice cream for a fast, impromptu dessert.

Someone once defined eternity as "a ham and two people." If you overestimated how much your relatives and friends could make their way through, you may be looking at several hammy days yet. Rather than feeling like leftovers, this dish with its tangy sauce is like something you'd create from scratch. A food processor makes the job much easier. If you don't own one, this recipe is excellent practice for your knife skills.

Preheat the oven to 350°F (180°C).

Mix together the ham, crackers, milk, egg, and pepper. Shape into 1-inch (2.5-cm) balls, and place in a deep ovenproof dish.

Whisk together the brown sugar, vinegar, water, and mustard until smooth. Pour over the ham balls. Cover the dish and bake for 1 hour, turning halfway through.

**PRESENTATION IS EVERYTHING**
Serving sliced apples browned in butter on the side, baked potatoes, and coleslaw gives this dish the appropriate retro diner feel.

## Hammi-Balls with Mustard Sauce

SERVES 4

1 lb (500 g) finely chopped ham
½ cup (125 mL) crushed crackers or dry breadcrumbs
½ cup (125 mL) milk
1 egg
freshly ground pepper to taste
½ cup (125 mL) brown sugar
¼ cup (60 mL) cider vinegar
¼ cup (60 mL) water
1 Tbsp (15 mL) Dijon mustard, or to taste

Moroccan Meatball
Tagine with Figs and
Winter Vegetables

## Moroccan Meatball Tagine with Figs and Winter Vegetables

SERVES 4

1 lb (500 g) ground lamb, seasoned with ½ tsp (2 mL) each of ground coriander, cumin, and cayenne pepper to taste; or 1 lb (500 g) merguez sausage, skinned
⅓ cup (75 mL) flour (approx.)
1 Tbsp (15 mL) olive oil
1 tsp (5 mL) finely chopped garlic
½ tsp (2 mL) paprika
¼ tsp (1 mL) dried thyme
1 tsp (5 mL) ground cumin
1 tsp (5 mL) ground coriander
1 tsp (5 mL) dried mixed ...
2 cups (500 mL) diced root vegetables
1½ cups (375 mL) cubed onions
1 cup (250 mL) chicken stock
½ cup (125 mL) red wine
1 cup (250 g) dried figs
½ cup (125 mL) chopped ...
1 cup (250 mL) canned diced ...
¼ cup (60 mL) chopped cilantro

*Fragrant with kasbah spices and dense with belly-warming root veggies, this dish is fantastic on a wintry night. Couscous goes best with it; rice is good too. Either way, sprinkle a little finely grated lemon rind over the top.*

Shape the lamb mixture into 1-inch (2.5-cm) meatballs and roll them in the flour.

Heat the olive oil in a large skillet and add the meatballs. Brown on all sides, about 10 minutes. Set the meatballs aside.

Add the garlic and spices to the skillet, and cook for 1 minute. Add the root vegetables and onions, and cook until slightly browned. Pour in the chicken stock and wine, and bring to a boil. Reduce the heat, and add the figs and tomatoes. Cover and simmer for 20 to 30 minutes or until the vegetables are almost tender. Add the meatballs, and continue cooking for 10 minutes or until the meatballs are heated through.

Sprinkle with the chopped cilantro.

**PRESENTATION IS EVERYTHING**
Bring out your traditional tagine dish with its conical lid if you have one.

Poulet à la diable is one of my favorite dishes; chicken smeared with mustard and dried chili peppers, egged and crumbed, and baked in the oven. There, all the flavors are on the outside. Here they're on the inside. If you can't get your hands on ground chicken, use ground turkey instead. Serve with creamy mashed potatoes and sautéed cherry tomatoes (see page 113).

Preheat the oven to 375°F (190°C).

Mix the ground chicken, mustard, and chili peppers. Roll into 1-inch (2.5-cm) balls. Chill for 2 hours.

Beat the egg with a fork in a flat soup bowl. Tip the breadcrumbs onto a plate. Dip each ball in the egg and then in the crumbs so that it's completely coated. Place the balls on a rimmed baking sheet and dab with the butter. Bake on the middle shelf of the oven for 25 to 30 minutes or until cooked through.

**PRESENTATION IS EVERYTHING**
Heap the chicken balls on a brown pottery plate and top with a sprig of parsley. Arrange sautéed cherry tomatoes (page 113) around the rim.

## Devilish Chicken Balls

SERVES 4

1 lb (500 g) ground chicken
1 Tbsp (15 mL) coarse Dijon mustard
½ tsp (2 mL) dried chili peppers, or to taste
1 egg
½ cup (125 mL) fresh breadcrumbs
2 Tbsp (30 mL) softened butter

# Fruit Balls

# Melon Ball-et

SERVES 6 TO 8

1 watermelon
1 cantaloupe
1 honeydew melon
green or red seedless grapes,
  blueberries, or cherries
  (optional)

*Fresh, healthy, colorful, and hugely impressive, this dish is a killer dessert for summer. It's relatively cheap to make, and you can prepare it in the morning, then forget about it until serving time. Once you've got the knack of performing the melon ballet, it becomes a summer mainstay. Melon baller mandatory—to give it that professional look.*

Using a sharp, thin-bladed knife, score the skin of the watermelon in a zigzag right around, about 2 inches (5 cm) from the top. Go round again, deepening the zigzags until you can lift off the top in I piece. Set the top aside.

Using a melon baller, scoop the watermelon's innards into a large bowl, discarding seeds as you do so (or use a seedless watermelon). Keep scooping until you are down to the inner pale skin. Use a sharp knife to neaten the inside and the top of the melon.

Halve and seed the remaining melons, and cut as many balls as you can from them. Add to the watermelon balls. Tumble the mixture around, add the other fruits (if you're using them), and gently mix again.

Fill the watermelon shell with the fruit mixture. Replace the top by matching the zigzag cuts, cover with plastic wrap, and refrigerate, along with any leftover fruit, until serving time. Bring to the table on a large platter, and don't lift the lid until you have everyone's attention.

**THE INDISPENSABLE MELON BALLER**
The melon baller is one gadget that's definitely worth getting. Most kinds have a scoop at each end; they let you create spheres of different sizes. While the melon baller's primary use is for melons, you'll also find it handy for cutting ripe avocados and making chocolate truffles.

**PRESENTATION IS EVERYTHING**
Serve with ice cream or lightly whipped cream, and cookies.

*Delicious on their own. For a treat, serve these cherries with French vanilla ice cream or a slice of pound cake or any combination thereof. Leave them in the fridge until 20 minutes before you want to bring them out. Double dip them in chocolate up to a day ahead.*

Line a platter or baking sheet with waxed paper. Pour the chocolate sprinkles into a bowl.

Melt the chocolate in a double boiler until smooth. Remove from the heat, reheating if necessary so that the chocolate is just melted. Dip each cherry into the melted chocolate so that it's completely covered. Then dip it quickly into the bowl of chocolate sprinkles. Place on the platter or baking sheet.

# Double Chocolate-Dipped Cherries

SERVES 4

¼ cup (60 mL) chocolate sprinkles
6 oz (175 g) chopped semi-sweet chocolate
25 to 30 large fresh cherries, complete with stems

**Grapes Glacés**

# Grapes Glacés

SERVES 4 AS A POST-DINNER NIBBLE

1 cup (250 mL) green or red
   seedless grapes

*The first time I had these frozen confections, they blew me away with their class and simplicity. Welsh-born John Bishop runs a very successful and eponymous restaurant in Vancouver. He serves these at the conclusion of dinner. This amount is sufficient for a delightful little nibble after you've had dessert. Larger quantities make a chillingly lovely ending on their own, outdoors on a warm summer evening, especially with a platter of ripe cheeses.*

Wash, dry, and de-stem the grapes. Place them on waxed paper on a plate in the freezer until serving time.

**PRESENTATION IS EVERYTHING**

Stack a combination of green and red grapes glacé in a little pyramid in a martini glass (which you had the foresight to also place in the freezer).

# Baked Apples

SERVES 4

*On my list of fail-safe wintertime desserts, baked apples come first. Mincemeat, chopped dried fruit—almost any mixture of fruit and nuts can be the core. Once I even used up chunks of leftover Christmas pudding. Be careful about the type of apples you pick. Some hold their shape when you bake them, others don't (see sidebar). A melon baller is handy for coring the apples.*

4 apples (see sidebar)
½ cup (125 mL) chopped nuts
½ cup (125 mL) raisins
2 Tbsp (30 mL) lemon juice
1 tsp (5 mL) lemon rind
⅓ cup (75 mL) brown sugar (approx.)
½ cup (125 mL) water (approx.)

Preheat the oven to 350°F (180°C).

Core each apple, leaving it whole. Cut around the middle of each with a sharp knife just to pierce the skin. Place in a baking dish just large enough to hold all 4 of them.

Combine the nuts, raisins, lemon juice, lemon rind, and 2 Tbsp (30 mL) of the brown sugar. Stuff the apples with the mixture.

Mix together the remaining brown sugar and the water, and drizzle over and around the apples. Cover with foil and bake for 15 minutes. Add more water if the liquid around them is starting to dry out. Taste the liquid too—apple sweetness varies—you may want to stir in a little more brown sugar. Bake for another 15 minutes or until the apples are cooked through.

**PRESENTATION IS EVERYTHING**
Cream, ice cream, or custard sauce are all amiable companions for this homey dessert.

**PICKING THE PROPER APPLES**
Cooked, certain varieties of apple like McIntosh turn to mush. They're still edible, but esthetically not what you want (although great for applesauce). If you're baking apples, look for Granny Smith or Braeburn or Golden Delicious. If you're lucky enough to come across obscure varieties of heirloom apples at a farmers' market, your best bet is to ask the grower which are best for cooking.

# Golden Creamy Apricot Globes

MAKES ABOUT 36

1 cup (250 mL) cream cheese or
   mascarpone
⅔ cup (150 mL) blanched
   almonds, coarsely chopped
2 cups (500 mL) dried apricots

*Cheese and dried fruit are natural partners—the salt, tang, and nuttiness of the one playing up the deep sweetness of the other. Whenever I make up a cheese platter, I add dried figs or apricots and nuts. The combination of sweet and salt and crunch really works. These apricot treats, I must admit, came into being as I was tidying up after a long dinner with friends. One of those "what would happen if . . ." moments. There was a dried apricot and there was a hunk of soft cheese. Buy the best dried apricots you can find. Dried up wrinklies won't work.*

Mix the cheese and almonds together in a small bowl. Carefully open up each apricot and stuff it with the mixture. Close the apricot and mold it into the shape of a globe, making sure that none of the cheese mixture escapes. Arrange the filled apricots on a platter, cover with plastic wrap, and refrigerate.

Bring to room temperature 1 hour before serving.

**PRESENTATION IS EVERYTHING**
Serve alongside a wedge of roquefort with digestive biscuits, or on their own with thin almond cookies.

*I have a passion for classic digestive biscuits, especially in combination with a sharp blue cheese—such as roquefort or Bleu d'Auvergne—and dried figs. You need fat, fleshy figs for this dish; the wizened kind won't do the trick. Try a Greek delicatessen rather than your supermarket.*

Mash the cheese, adding as much of the whipping cream as needed (if any) to make a smooth, stiff paste.

Trim the pointed end from each fig with a sharp knife. Using a spoon, carefully press down on the fig to create a small space (if necessary, remove a little of the fig's interior) and fill it with the cheese mixture. Press the top of the fig down and shape it into a ball, making sure that the cheese doesn't ooze out.

Serve immediately, or refrigerate and bring to room temperature 45 minutes before serving.

**PRESENTATION IS EVERYTHING**

If you have fig leaves, cover a plate with them. If not, vine leaves work well too.

## Figgy Puddings

MAKES ABOUT 20

⅔ cup (150 mL) blue cheese or
    goat cheese
¼ cup (60 mL) whipping cream
    (optional)
2 cups (500 mL) dried figs

# Blueberry Cobblers

SERVES 4

¾ cup (175 mL) water
⅓ cup (75 mL) sugar
1 Tbsp (15 mL) cornstarch
3 cups (750 mL) fresh or frozen
   blueberries (see sidebar)
1 tsp (5 mL) cinnamon
3 Tbsp (45 mL) plus 1 tsp
   (5 mL) butter
1 cup (250 mL) flour
1½ tsp (7 mL) baking powder
¼ tsp (1 mL) salt
⅓ cup (75 mL) milk or whipping
   cream

*Look how far along you are in this book, and how many suspect jokes have you seen? None. Until now. The many opportunities offered by the words "blue" and "balls" and the old English slang term "cobblers" were almost impossible to resist—like this homey dessert. By the way, the name "cobbler" came about because the surface of this dessert looks something like cobblestones. You can make this dessert with wild blackberries too.*

Preheat the oven to 425°F (220°C).

Combine the water, sugar, and cornstarch in a saucepan over medium heat. Mix well and bring to a boil, stirring until the mixture thickens. Remove from the heat and add the blueberries.

Butter a 6-cup (1.5-L) baking dish. Pour in the blueberry mixture, sprinkle with the cinnamon, and dab with 1 tsp (5 mL) of the butter.

Combine the flour, baking powder, and salt in a bowl. Melt the remaining 3 Tbsp (45 mL) of butter and mix together with the milk in a separate bowl.

Add the milk mixture to the flour mixture, and stir just until the dough forms a ball. Do not overmix. Drop the dough by 1-Tbsp (15-mL) dollops onto the blueberry mixture.

Bake in the middle of the oven on a baking sheet for 25 to 30 minutes or until golden-brown.

**PRESENTATION IS EVERYTHING**
Have a jug of whipping cream ready . . .

**FREEZING BLUEBERRIES**
Buy loads of fresh blueberries in season. Freeze them on cookie sheets, then tip them into plastic bags to keep frozen until needed.

*I have a deep hatred for useless gadgets, but nothing would part me from my ice cream maker. It's the easy, non-electric Donvier kind. Keeping the central cylinder in the freezer means we can make frozen treats any time we want. This sorbet technique works with most fruit. One can of fruit plus very little time equals an elegant and refreshing dessert. Sounds like a good deal to me.*

# Lychees with Lychee Sorbet

SERVES 4

one 14-oz (398-mL) can
   lychees, drained, juice
   reserved
4 small sprigs of mint

Refrigerate the lychees until needed.

Make the lychee juice into a sorbet using an ice cream maker. Or pour it into a pie plate, freeze it, break it up, and refreeze it. Bring to room temperature shortly before serving.

Using an ice cream scoop, place 1 boule of lychee sorbet into each of 4 sundae glasses. Top with the chilled lychees and garnish with the mint.

**PRESENTATION IS EVERYTHING**

If you use halved apricots instead of the lychees, and use plates instead of sundae glasses, you have a dessert that looks somewhat like a fried egg. Kids appreciate this. Adults with a sense of humor will too.

# Oranges Plain and Simple

SERVES 4

4 oranges
4 small sprigs of mint or lemon
  balm

*James Barber, otherwise known as TV's "Urban Peasant," has taught hundreds of thousands to cook in umpteen countries. Food fashions have come and gone since he began writing cookbooks in the 1970s, but what has always guided his approach is simplicity. He showed me the technique behind this easy but effective dessert once—and I've never forgotten it. You can make it for 50 people or for 2. It always works and invariably someone asks what the secret ingredient is. There isn't one.*

Using a small sharp knife, slice ½ inch (1 cm) off the bottom of each orange so that the flesh is revealed. Discard these slices. Cut a ¾-inch (2-cm) slice off each top—set these slices to one side.

Using the same knife, and holding the orange over a bowl to catch the juices, cut around the inside of the orange to remove as much of the flesh as possible. What you now have is an orange open at both ends.

Take the top slice of an orange, turn it upside down, and insert it all the way down into the orange so that it forms a new "bottom." Repeat with the other oranges.

Cut the orange flesh into small cubes, drizzle any saved juices over them, and fill the oranges. Garnish with the mint sprigs and refrigerate until serving time.

**PRESENTATION IS EVERYTHING**
This is a fabulous winter dessert when fresh fruit is in short supply. Arrange the oranges on a dark green or blue glass plate.

**BLOODY AMAZING!**
Any orange-based dessert is spectacular if you can get your hands on ruby-red-fleshed blood oranges.

# Oranges with Caramelized Zest

SERVES 4

4 large or 6 small oranges
1 cup (250 mL) sugar
½ cup (125 mL) water

*Here's another orange recipe that is much, much more than the sum of its parts. Who would think the simple combination of oranges, sugar, and water could result in a dessert this quietly impressive?*

Peel the oranges, leaving the white pith behind. Cut the rind into julienne strips.

Bring a large pot of water to the boil, drop in the strips of orange rind, and let them simmer for 10 minutes or until softened. Drain and rinse with cold water. Dry on a paper towel and set aside.

Peel the white pith off the oranges. Slice them thinly into a bowl so you don't lose any juices.

In a separate pan bring the sugar and water to a boil. Continue cooking until the sugar is completely dissolved. Continue boiling for 3 minutes. Add the rind and cook for 2 minutes longer. The syrup should thicken a little.

Remove the pan from the heat, let the candied orange rind and its syrup cool for 5 minutes, and spoon it over the orange slices.

Cover with plastic wrap and chill until serving time.

**PRESENTATION IS EVERYTHING**
A cluster of vivid blue borage flowers in the center looks spectacular.

With its meringue topping, this is rather reminiscent of retro desserts such as lemon meringue pie or baked Alaska. A bit 1950s. You feel you should serve it wearing a hostess apron. I usually make it with dried apricots, but you could use other dried fruit too: cranberries or cherries, or even raisins if that's all you have in the cupboard.

Preheat the oven to 300°F (150°C).

Cut a 1-inch (2.5-cm) slice from the top of each orange. Using a sharp narrow-bladed knife, cut out the pulp from each orange. Dice the orange pulp, and mix it with the apricots, raisins, chopped walnuts, and 1 Tbsp (15 mL) of the sugar. Fill the orange shells with the mixture.

Place the oranges in a casserole dish just large enough to hold them. Gently pour in water so that it comes ½ inch (1 cm) up the oranges. Bake for 45 minutes.

Beat the egg white with the remaining 1 Tbsp (15 mL) of sugar until it forms stiff peaks.

Remove the oranges from the oven. Top with the meringue and bake for a further 15 minutes.

Serve immediately.

**PRESENTATION IS EVERYTHING**
These oranges have a tendency to roll around, tipping off their meringue hats and spilling their contents. Contain them by holding them in small ramekins. If you then want to stand the ramekin at the center of a plate and add a couple of cookies on the side . . .

# Orange Surprises

SERVES 4

4 large oranges
2 Tbsp (30 mL) coarsely
   chopped apricots
1 Tbsp (15 mL) plus 1 tsp
   (5 mL) raisins
1 Tbsp (15 mL) plus 1 tsp
   (5 mL) chopped walnuts
2 Tbsp (30 mL) sugar
1 egg white

# Sweetie Balls

# Spicy Chocolate Truffles

MAKES ABOUT 30

½ cup (125 mL) whipping cream
2 Tbsp (30 mL) unsalted butter
1 Tbsp (15 mL) chili flakes, or
    to taste
½ lb (250 g) dark chocolate
½ cup (125 mL) unsweetened
    cocoa powder (approx.)

**TRUFFLE TRUTHS**
Truffles are easy to make. As
with any recipe, the better
the ingredients, the better the
results. Don't even think of
using some spurious chocolate
drink mix if the recipe calls for
unsweetened cocoa powder.

Four truffle recipes in one
book may seem like a lot, but
consider: what else functions
as a dessert, makes (as they say)
a handy hostess gift, and is a
wonderfully luxurious little
treat to bring out with after-
dinner coffee?

*One year my good friend Beverley's nephew, Jeff, made these as Christmas gifts. She got me the recipe, and told me that Jeff says adjusting the proportions of butter and cream will alter the texture. Less or more chilies will make them less or more spicy. You can also roll them in melted chocolate. Practice, practice, practice . . . I keep fantasizing about dropping one of these into a mug of blisteringly hot cocoa.*

Melt the cream and butter together in a pot over medium-low heat. Bring to a boil and reduce the heat. Add the chili flakes and simmer gently for 15 minutes. Strain the mixture into a bowl, discard the chili flakes, and return the mixture to the pot. Stir in the chocolate over low heat, and keep stirring continuously until it's melted. Refrigerate until hard (at least 1 hour).

Using a 1-tsp (5-mL) measure, scoop out some of the mixture, and quickly roll it between your hands into a ball. Roll in the cocoa powder to coat.

Either serve immediately, or store them in the fridge and bring to room temperature about 45 minutes before serving.

### PRESENTATION IS EVERYTHING

Seems to me that these would make a fitting conclusion to a Mexican dinner, either standing in for dessert or accompanying potent espressos afterward.

### TRUFFLE TRUTHS

Spring for good chocolate in a block—I like Valrhona. Use a double boiler to melt it. This doesn't mean buying one. It means, in my case, a small saucepan of chocolate bobbing around in a Corningware casserole filled with boiling water.

# Boozy Chocolate Truffles

MAKES ABOUT 30

½ lb (250 g) dark chocolate
½ cup (125 mL) whipping cream
¼ cup (60 mL) butter
2 Tbsp (30 mL) Cointreau,
    Kahlúa, Baileys, or other
    liqueur of your choice
½ cup (125 mL) unsweetened
    cocoa powder (approx.)

*Everyone's drinking habits are different. Our household always seems to end up with loads of bottles, all with pitifully little inside. You can use these odds and ends up by flambéing Christmas puddings, but a more delicious way is to incorporate them into chocolate truffles. No big secret to making them, except keeping your hands cool.*

Combine the chocolate, cream, and butter in a double boiler over low heat, and stir until completely melted. Stir in the booze and remove from the heat. Refrigerate the mixture until firm.

Using a 1-tsp (5-mL) measure, scoop up some of the chilled mixture and quickly roll it into a ball between your hands. Roll each ball in the cocoa.

Keep refrigerated. Bring to room temperature 30 minutes before serving.

**PRESENTATION IS EVERYTHING**
Little paper candy cups are ideal for housing truffles.

# Chocolate Cranberry Nut Truffles

**MAKES ABOUT 30**

½ lb (250 g) semi-sweet chocolate
½ cup (125 mL) cranberry sauce
2 Tbsp (30 mL) whipping cream
½ cup (125 mL) coarsely chopped walnuts, almonds, or hazelnuts (or a mix)
2 Tbsp (30 mL) cocoa powder (approx.)
2 Tbsp (30 mL) icing sugar (approx.)

*Like many recipes, this started life as a handwritten one that called for opening a can of cranberry sauce. Ever the thrifter, I've found it's great for using up the extra fresh cranberry sauce everyone makes at Christmas and Thanksgiving "just in case we don't have enough." Not to mention the walnuts hanging around after the holidays. No, you won't feel like eating truffles in January, so freeze the cranberry sauce till you're ready to make them.*

Combine the chocolate, cranberry sauce, and whipping cream in a saucepan over low heat. Cook, stirring constantly, until the chocolate is melted and the mixture is smooth. Fold in the nuts. Pour into a wide bowl and refrigerate until thickened, about 45 minutes.

Using a melon baller, scoop small balls of the mixture, and quickly roll them between your hands. Roll half the truffles in the cocoa, and the other half in the sugar.

Keep refrigerated. Bring to room temperature 30 minutes before serving.

**PRESENTATION IS EVERYTHING**

Mix half the nuts into half the chocolate mixture. Then roll the nut truffles in the remaining nuts, and the plain truffles in cocoa and/or sugar.

# English Trifle Truffles

MAKES ABOUT 30

1 cup (250 mL) finely chopped
   dried apricots
2 Tbsp (30 mL) sherry or
   brandy
½ cup (125 mL) whipping cream
½ lb (250 g) white chocolate
¼ cup (60 mL) ground almonds
3 Tbsp (45 mL) raspberry or
   strawberry jam
2 Tbsp (30 mL) Bird's Custard
   Powder
½ cup (125 mL) amaretti
   crumbs (approx.)

*A mainstay of my childhood Christmases, traditional English trifle is a baroque and rich concoction. Nostalgia was the catalyst for this particular truffle. Resist the temptation to sip too many glasses of sherry or brandy while you're making these. One sure test of sobriety is if you can say "English trifle truffles" very fast six times in a row.*

Combine the apricots and sherry in a bowl, and let stand for 10 minutes. Pour the cream into a small pan, place over medium heat, and bring to a boil. Remove from the heat and stir in the chocolate until melted. Add the undrained apricots, almonds, jam, and custard powder, and mix well. Refrigerate until the mixture is firm enough to handle, about 45 minutes.

Form into small balls and roll in the amaretti crumbs. Refrigerate until 1 hour before serving.

### PRESENTATION IS EVERYTHING
As served on the poshest dinner tables, English trifles are garnished with crystallized violets, halved blanched almonds, and/or stalks of crystallized angelica. You could fill in the gaps on your plate with those.

# Rum Balls

*Rather too easy to whip up on a whim, these deliciously alcoholic little morsels go down a treat. They're a nice pick-me-up with a mug of hot cocoa on a wintry day.*

Combine all the ingredients in a bowl and mix well. Shape into 1-inch (2.5-cm) balls. Using up to 3 Tbsp (45 mL) more icing sugar, roll the balls to cover them. Store in the fridge for 2 days if you like so that the flavors can develop.

If the rum balls look a little sticky, roll them again in more icing sugar before serving.

1 cup (250 mL) finely crushed vanilla wafers
1 cup (250 mL) finely chopped walnuts
¾ cup (175 mL) icing sugar (approx.)
⅓ cup (75 mL) rum

# White Chocolate Screw Balls

MAKES ABOUT 40

1½ cups (375 mL) coarsely
    chopped white chocolate
⅓ cup (75 mL) whipping cream
2 Tbsp (30 mL) vodka
2 tsp (10 mL) grated orange rind
1 cup (250 mL) icing sugar
    (approx.)

*Said to have got its name from the tool original-ly used to stir this traditional cocktail, the classic screwdriver is a simple and delicious alliance of vodka and orange juice. Add chocolate and you have an evil little piece of confectionery.*

Combine the white chocolate and whipping cream in a sauce-pan over low heat, and stir until the chocolate has melted and the mixture is smooth. Remove from the heat, and stir in the vodka and orange rind. Pour into a pie plate and refrigerate until the mixture firms up, about 2 hours.

Using a melon baller or 1-tsp (5-mL) measure, scoop up small balls of the mixture, and quickly form them into balls between your hands. Roll in the icing sugar. Keep refrigerated.

Bring to room temperature 30 minutes before serving.

PRESENTATION IS EVERYTHING
Serve accompanied by chilled orange sections.

*This is a "wow" of a dessert that's ludicrously easy to make. Use your favorite ice cream. Vanilla, strawberry, raspberry, espresso, mocha, double dark chocolate with chocolate chunks, peppermint, orange— it's hard to think of any flavor that isn't a delectable match with chocolate.*

# Giant Chocolate Ice Cream Truffles

SERVES 4

2 cups (500 mL) ice cream
6 oz (175 g) semi-sweet
chocolate, coarsely chopped

Scoop out the ice cream into tidy balls. Flatten them slightly so that they won't roll around, place on a plastic-wrap-covered plate, cover gently with more plastic wrap, and freeze until completely hard.

Melt the chocolate in a small saucepan over low heat. Gently drizzle the melted chocolate over the ice cream balls so that they're completely covered. Refreeze until 15 minutes before serving.

Peel the ice cream truffles off the plastic wrap. Snap off any hardened dribbles of chocolate. Serve immediately.

**PRESENTATION IS EVERYTHING**
Have some toasted, flaked almonds ready to sprinkle on top of the chocolate before it sets. A few dainty cookies or fan-shaped ice cream wafers, fresh raspberries, strawberries, or cherries . . .

# Profiteroles

SERVES 4

1 recipe choux pastry (see
    page 32)
1 egg, beaten
¾ cup (175 mL) whipped cream
    or ice cream
½ cup (125 mL) chocolate
    sauce, purchased or
    homemade

*This classic dessert shows up in bistros all over France. You can also fill the little choux pastry balls with ice cream. Use it straight from the freezer so that you get that delicious contrast of cold cream and warm chocolate.*

Preheat the oven to 425°F (220°C).

Using a piping bag with a ½-inch (1-cm) nozzle, make balls out of the choux pastry, approximately 1 inch (2.5 cm) in size. Place on a rimmed baking sheet and brush lightly with the beaten egg.

Bake on the middle shelf of the oven for 20 minutes. Reduce heat to 350°F (180°C) and bake for 10 minutes more. Slit the choux pastry balls and let cool on a rack.

At serving time, split each ball, fill with whipped cream, and arrange on 4 dessert plates or flat soup plates.

Meanwhile, warm the chocolate sauce in a small saucepan. Pour the sauce over the balls and serve immediately.

**TOWER OF BA-BALLS**
With its airy crown of spun sugar, the classic *croquembouche*—a conical tower of choux pastry balls held together with caramel—makes a spectacular centerpiece for an extravagant dessert buffet. Its name translates as "crunch in the mouth."

*The classic recipe is a cake covered in whipped cream. I think this insanely simple but highly impressive multi-layered ice cream dessert is far more deserving of the name.*

Line a 3-cup (750-mL) pudding basin with plastic wrap. Bring the vanilla ice cream to room temperature, and spread a thick layer on the inside of the basin. Freeze for 1 hour.

Repeat with the raspberry sorbet and chocolate ice cream. Freeze until serving time.

Remove the "snowball" from the basin, peel off the plastic wrap, and cut the dessert into wedges.

**PRESENTATION IS EVERYTHING**
Place a garland of fresh raspberries around the base of the dessert and one on the top.

# Boule de Neige

SERVES 6

1½ cups (375 mL) vanilla ice cream
1 cup (250 mL) raspberry sorbet
½ cup (125 mL) chocolate ice cream

**OTHER ICE CREAM COMBOS**
Vanilla, raspberry, and chocolate is only one possibility. Try chocolate, coffee, and mocha. What you're after is both color contrast and flavor compatibility. You can even create a pretend watermelon with lime sorbet on the outside and a center of bright red strawberry sorbet studded with chocolate chips.

# Viennese Sugar Balls

MAKES ABOUT 30

1¾ cups (425 mL) icing sugar
  (approx.)
1 cup (250 mL) butter, softened
1 cup (250 mL) ground,
  blanched almonds
1½ tsp (7 mL) vanilla essence
½ tsp (2 mL) almond essence
2½ cups (625 mL) flour

*Cloudy with their coating of icing sugar, these yummy little cookies show up under different names: Mexican wedding cakes, pecan butterballs. I prefer Viennese Sugar Balls because it suggests young ladies, exhausted by too many go-rounds of the Blue Danube, seeking sustenance on the dance floor sidelines. Handle the dough gently to keep the delicate texture these cookies are known for. You can also make them with pecans or hazelnuts instead of almonds.*

Preheat the oven to 350°F (180°C).

Cream together ¾ cup (175 mL) of the icing sugar and the butter. Stir in the ground almonds, and the vanilla and almond essences. Gradually stir in the flour until completely mixed. Refrigerate the dough for 1 hour.

Roll the dough out to 1 inch (2.5 cm) thick, and cut into 1-inch (2.5-cm) squares. Using your hands, gently roll each square into a ball. Place the balls 1½ inches (4 cm) apart on a greased, rimmed baking sheet. Bake for 15 minutes or until lightly golden. Remove from the oven and let cool on a rack.

Roll in the remaining icing sugar until coated all over. Store in a lidded tin with waxed paper between the layers.

**PRESENTATION IS EVERYTHING**

Giving homemade cookies is a nice thing to do. Set each one in a small paper case.

**HOW TO BLANCH ALMONDS**

You can buy blanched almonds everywhere, but if you can only find almonds still in their skins (or even in their shells; you can remove the shells with nutcrackers), drop them in boiling water for 5 minutes or until their brown skins swell. Drain, let cool enough to handle, pop them out of their skins, and dry on paper towels.

# Gateau St. Honoré de Balls-ac

SERVES 6 TO 8

1 cup (250 mL) flour
¼ tsp (1 mL) salt
¼ cup (60 mL) butter
1 egg yolk
2 Tbsp (30 mL) cold water
  (approx.)
1 recipe choux pastry (see
  page 32)
4 eggs
½ cup (125 mL) sugar
3 Tbsp (45 mL) cornstarch
¼ tsp (1 mL) vanilla
1 cup (250 mL) milk
½ cup (125 mL) whipping cream
3 Tbsp (45 mL) water
3 Tbsp (45 mL) sliced almonds,
  lightly toasted

*Balzac, or—as we should think of him—Balls-ac, was a 19th-century French author. He is also the patron saint of pâtissiers. If you live in France, this puff pastry-ball-decorated cake is what your family delights you with on your birthday. It's much more straightforward to make than it sounds, but it does take time.*

Preheat the oven to 400°F (200°C).

Combine ¾ cup (175 mL) of the flour and the salt in a bowl, then rub in the butter until the mixture resembles fine breadcrumbs. Add the egg yolk and enough of the cold water to make a stiff dough. Press the dough together with your fingertips. Refrigerate the dough while you make the choux pastry.

On a lightly floured surface, roll the chilled dough (for the base) into an 8-inch (20-cm) round, and place on a rimmed baking sheet.

Using a piping bag with a ½-inch (1-cm) nozzle, pipe a circle of choux pastry around the edge of the dough base. Beat 1 of the eggs, and brush over the choux pastry circle.

With the remaining choux pastry, pipe 20 small balls onto a separate baking sheet.

Bake both the base and the choux pastry balls for 15 minutes. Lower the temperature to 275°F (140°C), and continue to bake for 12 minutes, or until the choux pastry circle around the base rises and is golden brown.

Slit the choux pastry balls to release the steam, and leave them to cool on a rack.

For the pastry cream, separate 2 of the eggs, setting the whites aside. In a medium bowl, beat together the yolks, the 1 remaining whole egg, and ¼ cup (60 mL) of the sugar. Stir in the remaining ¼ cup (60 mL) of the flour, the cornstarch, and vanilla.

Heat the milk in a pan over low heat until it is almost simmering, then slowly beat it into the egg mixture. Return the mixture to a clean pan and bring to the boil, stirring continually. Boil until the mixture thickens (2 to 3 minutes). Pour the milk mixture into a clean bowl. Cover the surface with buttered parchment paper and leave to cool.

Whip the cream until stiff. Spoon into a piping bag and fill the choux balls.

Combine the remaining ¼ cup (60 mL) of the sugar and the water in a heavy-bottomed saucepan, and heat until the sugar dissolves. Boil until the syrup turns pale yellow. Remove from the heat and dip the base of each ball in the syrup. Position the balls evenly around the edge of the choux pastry circle (you may have some left over). Spoon a little syrup over each ball.

Whisk the 2 reserved egg whites until stiff and fold into the cooled milk mixture, also adding any leftover whipped cream. Fill the center of the gateau with the pastry cream.

Decorate with the sliced almonds. Serve any spare, cream-filled balls on the side.

**ALL ABOUT ST. HONORÉ**
He's not only the patron saint of bakers and pastry chefs, but St. Honoré is also the patron saint of confectioners, candle makers, and florists. Three other factoids: he lived in the 7th century; he was the Bishop of Amiens; his feast day is May 16.

# Chocolate-Hazelnut Mousse with Ferrero Rocher Topping

SERVES 4

1 cup (250 mL) whipping cream
⅓ cup (75 mL) Nutella
4 Ferrero Rocher chocolates
2 Tbsp (30 mL) toasted,
   chopped hazelnuts

*I am nuts about Nutella—and so are most people in France, judging both from the walls of Nutella jars in Gallic supermarkets and its popularity as a crêpe filling. Chocolate and hazelnuts mixed together is a felicitous combination. Here I've used it as the base for simple but obscenely rich little mousses, then upped the calories even more by placing Ferrero Rocher chocolates on top.*

Combine the whipping cream and Nutella in a large bowl. Whisk until soft peaks begin to form. Spoon into 4 little bowls. Refrigerate until serving time.

Just before serving, center a Ferrero Rocher chocolate on each little mousse, and sprinkle the toasted hazelnuts around it.

### PRESENTATION IS EVERYTHING

You can also spoon this dessert into a large bowl, place the Ferrero Rochers in artistic places, sprinkle on the hazelnuts, and shave a little dark chocolate overall.

### NUTELLA: A HISTORY

The predecessor of Nutella was invented in the 1940s by an Italian named Pietro Ferrero. This was wartime, so to eke out the chocolate he added hazelnuts, which were abundant in his native Piedmont. Today, globally, Nutella outsells peanut butter. The same company, as you've possibly guessed, makes Ferrero Rocher.

### MUSIC OF THE SPHERES

A popular treat in Austria, Mozartkugeln translates as "Mozart balls." Inside their chocolate coating are nougat and marzipan.

*Indian desserts are often ball-shaped, and also very rich. I'd serve these treats after a fairly light, and not necessarily Indian, meal. Curry plus rasgulla might be too much of a good thing. Grilled chicken with Indian spices and a huge salad would be a better lead-up.*

# Rasgulla (Cardamom Milk Balls)

MAKES ABOUT 30

4 cups (1 L) whole milk
¼ cup (60 mL) lemon juice
1 pinch of saffron
½ tsp (2 mL) ground
   cardamom, or to taste
3 cups (750 mL) water
1 cup (250 mL) sugar

Pour the milk into a pan, add the lemon juice and saffron, and bring to a boil over medium heat. Let stand until the milk separates into curds and whey.

Line a strainer with 2 layers of cheesecloth. Pour in the separated milk, and let drain for 15 minutes so that you have solid chunks.

Blend the chunks with the cardamom into a thick paste. Shape into 1-inch (2.5-cm) balls.

Fill a wide skillet with the water to a depth of about 2 inches (5 cm). Stir in the sugar, bring to a boil, and cook until the sugar is completely dissolved. Reduce the heat until the mixture is just simmering. Add the milk balls and let cook for 30 minutes.

Let the *rasgulla* cool in the syrup and serve cold.

### PRESENTATION IS EVERYTHING

Arrange the *rasgulla* in a shallow bowl, and decorate with a few sequins of that edible silver leaf you can buy at Indian groceries.

**CELEBRATORY SWEETMEATS**

Invitations to an Indian wedding are traditionally delivered with *ludoos*. These are balls of chickpea dough dyed a festive pink. They are then cooked in sugar syrup, before relatives and friends gather around to roll them by hand. The technique is handed down from one generation to the next.

# Halloween Eye Balls

MAKES 24

one 10-oz (300-g) package of
   large marshmallows
¼ cup (60 mL) butter
6 cups (1.5 L) Rice Krispies
24 Hershey's chocolate kisses
blood-red decorator icing

*Sick, sick, sick. Kids love them of course. Don't bother to hand these out at the door unless you know the witches and werewolves concerned. All modern children are firmly instructed to throw away anything that even vaguely looks as though it's made by a stranger's hand.*

Butter a large piece of waxed paper and set it on the counter.

Stir the marshmallows and butter together in a large pot set over a second pot of boiling water until they are completely melted and mixed. Stir in the Rice Krispies until completely coated. Tip the mixture onto the waxed paper and spread it out with a spatula.

When cool enough to handle, rub your hands with butter and shape the mixture into 24 balls. Press a chocolate kiss, pointed side down, into each ball. Allow to cool further.

Once the eyeballs are firm, decorate artistically with the icing to create bloodshot eyes. Let dry and store covered at room temperature.

**PRESENTATION IS EVERYTHING**
A few of these in a recycled chocolate box are a lovely surprise for some-one anticipating ordinary cookies or candies.

_These cookies aren't too sweet, which is good. Their heritage is French, which possibly explains why. In fact, with enough fresh fruit to salve your conscience and a big bowl of café au lait, you would have yourself a very Parisian and self-indulgent little weekend breakfast._

Preheat the oven to 325°F (160°C).

Mix together the flour, cocoa powder, and cinnamon in a large bowl.

Beat together the butter and sugar in a separate bowl until creamy. Stir in the vanilla essence.

Stir the butter mixture into the flour mixture until it forms a smooth dough. Shape into 1-inch (2.5-cm) balls, and place on a baking sheet lined with parchment paper. Bake for 15 minutes on the middle shelf or until slightly browned on top.

Let cool on the baking sheet and store in an airtight container.

**PRESENTATION IS EVERYTHING**
Sift the lightest possible cloud of icing sugar over a plateful.

## Chocolate Balls

MAKES ABOUT 40

1½ cups (375 mL) flour
⅓ cup (75 mL) cocoa powder
½ tsp (2 mL) ground cinnamon
1 cup (250 mL) softened butter
⅓ cup (75 mL) icing sugar
1 tsp (5 mL) vanilla essence

*Index*

# A

# B

# C

Balls!